They Paid Me for This?

Dave Coar

They Paid Me for This?

Stories from over Three Decades in Law Enforcement

David Coppage

*BOOK*LOGIX®
Alpharetta, GA

The author has tried to recreate events, locations, and conversations from his/her memories of them. In some instances, in order to maintain their anonymity, the author has changed the names of individuals and places. He/she may also have changed some identifying characteristics and details such as physical attributes, occupations, and places of residence.

ISBN: 978-1-61005-773-8
Library of Congress Control Number: 2016910947

10 9 8 7 6 5 4 3 2   0 9 2 7 1 6

Printed in the United States of America

∞This paper meets the requirements of ANSI/NISO Z39.48-1992 (Permanence of Paper)

To my wife, Melissa, and our two children, Casey and Kyle.

It is not the critic who counts; not the man who points out how the strong man stumbles, or where the doer of deeds could have done them better. The credit belongs to the man who is actually in the arena, whose face is marred by dust and sweat and blood; who strives valiantly; who errs, who comes up short again and again, because there is no effort without error and shortcoming; but who does actually strive to do the deeds; who knows great enthusiasms, the great devotions; who spends himself in a worthy cause; who at the best knows in the end the triumph of high achievement, and who at the worst, if he fails, at least fails while daring greatly, so that his place shall never be with those cold and timid souls who know neither victory nor defeat.

"The Man in the Arena" speech by Theodore Roosevelt at the
Sorbonne, Paris, France
April 23, 1910

Contents

Acknowledgments

SPECIAL THANKS TO ALL OF THE MEN AND WOMEN THAT I HAD THE pleasure and privilege of serving with over my thirty-three-year career in law enforcement. That list is long, but I would like to pay particular homage to Grady Arnette, Tom Parnell, Mark Whitaker, Mike Coker, Irma Lisenby, and Jeff Alexander of the Montgomery, Alabama, Police Department; Mike Rich, Steve Wunderlich, John Shirley, Brian Smith, Bill Velasco, Woody Kirk, and Steve Hayward of the US Customs Service; and Mark Woodall of the US Federal Air Marshal Service. I would also like to acknowledge the hard work and dedication from the BookLogix team, who was instrumental in helping me get this book published.

Introduction

ANYBODY WHO HAS SPENT A CAREER IN LAW ENFORCEMENT WILL be able to relate to many of the stories in this book. Many readers will only have an idea of what it is like to carry a gun for a living from TV and movie portrayals. That view, however, is not tied to reality. This book is one person's story (mine), and not too atypical from other law enforcement agents and officers who spent most of their adult life serving their fellow man, doing what they were called to do. I hope this memoir will provide the reader with an inside look at what it's like to be a cop, with a little more insight into some behind-the-scenes observations (not all positive) of the agencies I had the privilege of working for.

I. WHY WE DO THIS JOB

FIVE MILES OFF THE COAST OF CAPE FLORIDA, JUST A LITTLE NORTH of Key Largo, the radio broke the extreme silence.

"Mike-one-nine," came the call over the radio.

We were one of several marine (or "Mike") units taking part in "Operation Hammerhead." Several US Customs speedboats (known to us as "go-fast" boats) were lined up off the southern coast of Florida about five miles apart. We were waiting to intercept anyone attempting to smuggle drugs into the US via the Bahamian Highway. This was a forty-mile stretch of water between the Bahamian island of Bimini (and other tiny rock outcroppings that helped form the Bahama Island chain) and any number of marine entry points into South Florida.

For several years, smugglers had been arranging airdrops of cocaine and marijuana that had been flown over from Colombia via various intermediate waypoints. Often utilizing single- or twin-engine planes, the smugglers would drop their loads to waiting boats sitting off some rock formation somewhere in the middle of the Bahamian chain. These planes would fly to a prearranged latitude/longitude coordinate in the ocean. They would then find a waiting boat that had used their onboard Loran-C unit to pinpoint the spot in the vast ocean where the drop was to take place. Once the smugglers in their boat had loaded the "cargo," they would then make the forty-five-minute-

1

to-an-hour jaunt across the Atlantic and into the US through one of the dozens of inlets across South Florida that provided access to the Intracoastal Waterway. Once a boat reached the "inside," there were dozens of canals and Biscayne Bay that provided the smugglers with easy access to literally hundreds of docks. Once docked, they could then offload their drugs to a waiting vehicle and into the marketplace of South Florida, always starving for more and more illicit drugs.

This operation was one of many marine operations that were constantly being conducted as part of Vice President George H. W. Bush's War on Drugs, a "war" that President Reagan had put him in charge of. I came onboard in 1986 at the beginning of this declared war. US Customs was leading the battle against drug smuggling, and stemming the flow of drugs being smuggled into the US via the marine environment was a critical piece to winning this war. The most essential tool at our disposal was the go-fast boat—ocean-racing boats big and fast enough to keep up with the boats being used by the smugglers and equipped with agents, weapons, and enough ammo to overcome any threat that may be encountered on the high seas when (or if) we ran across one of them. The boats in the US Customs arsenal were varied. Some were smuggler boats that had been previously seized and were now in use by the government. Others were specifically built for us and designed to be able to cut through waves and keep up with whatever the dopers were using.

Many regarded famed boatbuilder Don Aronow as the world's most accomplished designer and builder of ocean racers. He had been approached by government officials about designing a heavy-duty go-fast for use by US Customs in the War on Drugs. The finished product would come to be known as *Blue Thunder*. This was a twin-pontoon catamaran, thirty-nine feet long and twelve feet wide with twin 450-

horsepower inboard/outboard engines. At about $300,000 apiece, this was US Customs's secret weapon in the never-ending (and never-winning) War on Drugs. This massive boat, weighing several tons, could slice through five- or six-foot waves with ease out in the Atlantic and run down just about anything the smugglers had.

This vessel quickly became the "face" of our efforts to stop the flow of drugs coming into the US via the marine environment. It also possibly cost Mr. Aronow his life. Leaving his manufacturing facility in Miami (in an area known as "Thunderboat Row" because of several boatbuilding facilities housed there), Mr. Aronow was stopped at a red light when a blue Lincoln pulled up alongside. The passenger in the Lincoln motioned for Mr. Aronow to roll down his window, as if he wanted to ask him something. When Mr. Aronow did, the passenger in the Lincoln opened fire with a semiautomatic handgun, killing Mr. Aronow instantly. Rumors began to circulate that the killing was in response to his agreement with the federal government to "help" them in their War on Drugs by designing and building *Blue Thunder*. This was never confirmed, as the killers escaped. More than a decade later, two career criminals pled no contest to the killing. One of these killers had been in a business dispute with Mr. Aronow at the time of the killing. Suffice to say, accurately assigning the motive for the killing is impossible.

Another go-fast used by us in this war was the Chris-Craft Stinger. This was the boat we were on during Operation Hammerhead. The Stinger was a very sleek thirty-nine-foot boat with twin 420-horsepower inboard/outboard engines. Not nearly as big and heavy as *Blue Thunder*, it could still negotiate quite nicely in rough seas and was much more maneuverable. It was three o'clock in the morning and the cloud cover on this night blocked out what light would have been provided by the moon and stars. The seas were incredibly flat, and only a faint whisper was needed to communicate between me and the other two Customs agents onboard.

It would not be unusual to go an entire shift in one of these operations and never hear a peep from the radio. On this particular night, the Customs platform boat (a Boston whaler using very sophisticated radar equipment) had detected some type of movement in the general area where we sat. The radar operator could "see" on his radar screen each of the Customs boats lined up and down the coast. He radioed to inform us that there was a new "blip" appearing on his screen and that it was moving at a very slow pace in our general direction.

"Mike-one-nine," came the call to us.

"Mike-nineteen, go ahead," we replied.

"I've got a boat moving toward you about a mile to your east," the operator on the platform boat told us.

"Copy that," we said.

Many times in an operation like this, a radar "blip" turns out to be nothing more than an innocent fisherman or just someone out enjoying the peace and serenity of being out on the ocean on a night like this where the seas are so calm. The "blip" could also be something that we referred to as a "phantom wave," where there actually is no boat at all. But there is also the possibility that it's a real-life smuggler. And this is exactly what we signed up for. The heart rate goes up and breathing intensifies, all in anticipation of catching a smuggler.

A standard (and vitally indispensable) piece of equipment on a "Mike" unit was our night-vision device (NVDs or goggles). Our boat operator this evening was my friend Alan Childers. He and I were hired at the same time and had gone through the training academy at Glynco, Georgia, together. Glynco (actually located in Brunswick, Georgia, Glynn County, thus the name Glynco) was once a navy base that had been decommissioned back in the '70s and was due to be completely shut down. At the time, the government was looking for a place to set up a new training facility where most federal law enforcement training would take place. Jimmy Carter was president at the time, and being from Georgia himself, it only made sense to transform this old navy base into what would become the Federal Law Enforcement Training Center (FLETC). Agents who trained there would ultimately nickname the place "FLEA-TEC," primarily because of the gnats (or "flying teeth," as I like to refer to them) that assaulted you on a daily basis as you performed training exercises outside.

Tom Trotto (or "Double T," as we called him) was the third member of our crew this evening. He quickly handed me the NVDs. Alan was at the helm and getting everything ready should it be necessary to start the engines and move, while Tom retrieved the AR-15 rifle and made sure a round was chambered. NVDs are a sophisticated piece of equipment that can amplify light so faint that it cannot be detected by the human eye. The result is a very grainy view with a greenish hue and almost no depth perception. On this particular night, it was so dark you could barely see your hand in front of your face. All dashboard lights on the Stinger had to be off if there was any chance of seeing something on the horizon. I stared through the NVDs for several minutes, scanning the horizon. Suddenly, I could see a faint object moving slowly back and forth that appeared to be no more than two or three hundred yards away. I passed the goggles around so Alan and Tom could take a look, and for the next twenty minutes or so we just sat there in complete silence and watched.

As quietly as he could whisper, Alan keyed the mike on the Customs radio.

"Papa-100, this is Mike-one-nine. Target identified. Small boat, maybe twenty-footer, about two hundred yards to our east. Radio going silent. Will get back in a few."

"Roger that," replied Papa-100.

During that twenty-minute wait, we all donned our Customs "raid" jackets (blue windbreakers with large lettering that said "POLICE: US CUSTOMS"). Tom took his position on the back seat with the AR-15. I positioned myself front left and plugged in a handheld spotlight, and Alan put his right hand on the ignition key and left hand on the switch that turned on the blue light. I continued to watch through the NVDs and whispered faintly the target's position. "Fifty yards and closing." Then, "Twenty-five yards, directly off our bow. Still coming toward us."

We had already worked it out that I would hit the spotlight and simultaneously Alan would turn on the blue light and start the engines, anticipating that as soon as our existence was made known, the chase would be on. It followed absolutely true to form. When the target got within fifteen or twenty yards, I lit them up with the spotlight and the driver of the target boat immediately hit the gas and the chase began.

Tom grabbed the radio mike and informed everybody that we had initiated chase of the target boat and to respond accordingly.

The target boat was a relatively small twenty-two-foot go-fast, which at the time the chase began was weighed down with about two thousand pounds of marijuana bales. As they tried to elude us, the passenger began throwing the bales over the side of the boat while the driver zigzagged through the water, trying to get away. Alan kept the Stinger on their tail as I continually kept them lit up with the spotlight. After the last bale was thrown over, their boat became a little bit faster and easier to maneuver, but it became obvious it was not going to be able to run away from us.

At one point in the chase Alan pulled up directly beside their boat on their starboard side (the left, or portside, of our boat), literally just outside of my reach. As it was obvious they were not going to surrender, I pulled out my holstered Glock-19, semiautomatic 9mm and with the spotlight in my left hand still pointed at them, I began firing into the engine compartment at point-blank range. This did nothing to disable the engine nor convince the driver to give up.

He made a hard left turn and we momentarily separated by a few yards. Alan went left as well, and soon we were right on their tail again. It went back and forth like this for what seemed like hours, but was only a matter of a few minutes. As we began to run down the smugglers yet again from behind, the suspect quickly pulled back on his throttle that caused us to shoot by him on his right. Just before we were about to clear him, he turned hard right and hit the gas, attempting to swing behind us to get away. However, when he made this move, we had not completely cleared him and when he throttled up, the bow of his boat hit us directly in our back-left stern area. His pointed bow punctured through the fiberglass body of our Stinger and cut out a gaping hole in our engine compartment, just above the water line. A foot lower and we would have been sunk. Literally.

The violence of the impact was intense. Alan and I were positioned up front and the cushions of the front two standing-seats kept us from being thrown around. Poor Tom was not as fortunate. He had been in the back with nothing really to hold onto, and after impact I looked behind me to see if he was okay. I got a quick glimpse of him bouncing around like a pinball, trying to not lose his grip on the AR-15 rifle. Both boats were immediately dead in the water. I truly thought the chase was over at this point. Our boats were only a few feet apart, and I continued to train the spotlight on them. The suspect immediately began to recrank their engine in order to continue their attempt to flee. Alan also did the same, and moments later the chase was back on.

As we pulled up alongside yet again, the suspect driver began slamming his boat into ours as we went through the water side by side. He tacked hard left again to separate, and we ended up yet again gaining on them from behind. At this point in the chase, it became obvious that they were not going to give up. In fact, they had actually endangered our lives by using their boat as a weapon. I decided that shooting the suspect driver was the only way to safely end this chase. With my Glock still in hand, I rested my gun hand on the top of the windshield, and while still holding the spotlight with my left hand, I fired off five or six shots in the direction of the driver. Under the circumstances that existed, acquiring a good "sight picture" (looking through the gun sights and lining up the sights) was impossible. Moving at thirty or forty miles an hour and hopping waves while trying to keep the spotlight on the targets made it impossible to be accurate. I just pointed my gun in their direction and fired.

The suspect driver immediately dropped to the floor of his boat and out of sight.

"I think you hit 'em," yelled Alan.

A second or two later we saw a hand rise up into our view and grab the throttle and pull it back, stopping their boat. Both suspects then raised their hands in the air and surrendered. I immediately noticed a large amount of blood flowing down the left arm of the suspect driver. As it turned out, one of my shots had hit him in the hand he was using to hold the wheel and had completely blown off one of his fingers. That apparently was enough for him.

Post-arrest debriefing of the two smugglers uncovered the fact that they had been paid to transport the load of marijuana from the Bahamas to the US. They were supposed to meet another boat that would take possession of the load and bring it the rest of the way in. Many in law enforcement will say, "We only catch the dumb ones." These guys would certainly fall into that category. As it turned out, they were at the wrong rendezvous point. The boat they were supposed to meet was about five miles further up the coast!

Several months later their trial was held at the federal courthouse in Key West. Both suspects were convicted of smuggling and received twenty-year sentences. While the trial was going on, an interesting thing occurred. On the third day of the trial, some other agents and I were having breakfast at a local diner before that day's proceedings. Our waitress came over to pour us coffee and, before walking away, she said, "Those guys are guilty as hell." I looked up as she turned away and immediately recognized her as one of the jury members! This encounter, if reported to the judge, would most probably have been grounds for a mistrial. I looked over at the other guys and said, "That did not just happen." Nobody said a thing. They were convicted the following day after the jury deliberated for about an hour.

II. THE EARLY YEARS AND HOW IT ALL BEGAN

THIS ALL GOT STARTED FOR ME IN THE EARLY '70S. MY FAVORITE TV shows were *Adam-12* and *The Wild Wild West*. Most people look at TV depictions of police officers and think, "No way would I want to do that." For me, it was completely the opposite. I was enthralled by the idea of being a cop. Of course I knew that there was a certain degree of danger with that line of work, but that didn't deter me. It was the excitement that drew me in. I wanted to be a part of that. I knew from about age fourteen or fifteen that I wanted to be in law enforcement. As I got closer to graduating from high school in 1977, I began to consider different colleges to apply to. This was before the Internet or email, so I had to do everything the old-fashioned way—through snail mail. I got information from several colleges, but the one that stuck out to me was Troy State University in Troy, Alabama. What impressed me the most was the fact that they had a large criminal justice program. That's all I needed to see. I knew right then where I wanted to go.

After graduating from Troy in 1981 with a degree in criminal justice, I was hired as a police officer for the Montgomery, Alabama, Police Department (MPD). On the day of my final interview and polygraph exam before being offered a position, I remember sitting in the lobby of police headquarters waiting to be seen. As I sat there, a big, burly detective walked by me with a prisoner in tow that he had just arrested and was about to process in. I remember thinking to myself, *Now there is the quintessential example of an Alabama cop.* He was wearing a crumpled suit that looked slept in, a tie with traces of what he had for lunch, cowboy boots, a cowboy hat, and a toothpick hanging from his bottom lip. His name was J. W. Barnes and he, coincidentally, would later leave the MPD and follow me over to US Customs where he, too, enjoyed a long federal career.

Policing in the South during this time was quite the eye-opener for me. I was young, eager, and hungry to learn everything I could about this new career I had embarked on. My initial training was MPD's sixteen-week police academy. The training was rigorous and about half of those that started ended up dropping out and never made it to graduation. I made it through with the help of my good friend and classmate Mark Whitaker. Mark ended up retiring from the Alabama State Troopers after a long and successful career with them.

Montgomery's mayor at that time was Emory Folmar. Mayor Folmar was a true law and order mayor, and he loved the police department. He was also a Republican and friends with President Reagan. The majority of his critics in Montgomery were black Democrats who were always complaining about how his police officers were treating the black community. In hindsight, some of the criticism may have been justified, but most was not. We weren't that far removed from the racial divisions that existed in the South during the '60s and '70s, and the landscape was still fairly ripe for those who wanted to use race as a rallying point for dissent.

Mayor Folmar demanded excellence from his officers and did not tolerate incompetency. He didn't care what color you were. He just wanted his officers to act as professionals. There is no doubt that he ruled the department with an iron fist. In spite of this, there was a small number of "old-timers" that had been around a long time and had their own ideas on how to police the streets.

Thank God there were no smartphones back then with video capabilities! "Southern Justice" (as it was known) took place from time to time. Some officers tended to exact a little "pain" when taking someone into custody, depending on the circumstances surrounding the arrest. Now, I'm not condoning it, I'm just saying that it took place.

I was driving a patrol car one afternoon and was called by Detective Ralph Connor to meet him at a house to serve an arrest warrant on a lowlife that was being arrested for molesting a minor. We found him at home, upstairs in his bedroom. We took him into custody and I cuffed his hands behind his back. I walked down the stairs in front of Ralph, who was holding the suspect by his elbow. The stairs descended down a flight to a landing and then turned left and descended yet again into the living room. A brick wall was at the bottom of this flight of stairs at the end of the landing. Ralph was at the top of the stairs getting ready to walk down when I looked up at him.

I smacked the palm of my hand on the brick wall and said, "Hey, Ralphie, betcha can't hit this spot."

He knew immediately what I meant. From the top step he grabbed the suspect with both hands and as hard as he could, thrust him down the entire flight of stairs. His face and chest smashed into the brick wall next to where I stood. With his hands cuffed behind him, he had no chance to break his fall. He crumpled in a ball on the landing at my feet.

"Nice shot, Ralph," I said.

We had a pretty good laugh at that.

Being a cop on the street will make you a tougher person than you would have become otherwise. It's just a fact. Physical encounters with suspects you are trying to arrest occur quite frequently. Peer pressure requires you to respond accordingly. No cop wants to be seen as someone who will back down when a threat appears. You want your fellow offices to know they can count on you when things get a little dicey. Most of the friends of a cop are other cops, and most of the friends of a cop's spouse are other cops' spouses. It's just the way it is. It's part of the culture. Because cops hang out mostly with other cops, they don't want to be known as someone that will not be there for the other guy when things go bad.

My partner and I were on patrol one night on the west side of town. This part of Montgomery was a high-crime area and known to be pretty rough. Another patrol unit close-by called for assistance. They were trying to make an arrest in the middle of the street of a suspect that had outstanding warrants on him. About thirty people in this neighborhood were all out yelling at the cops, and the suspect was not cooperating. It had all the makings of a potential riot if the situation was not quickly controlled and the suspect removed.

We got there in a matter of minutes and I grabbed the shotgun as I exited the patrol car. My partner and I waded into the middle of the crowd and stood next to the two officers already there. The guy they were trying to arrest was jumping up and down, yelling at us and trying to get the crowd of people fired up. One of the other officers walked toward the suspect, holding his shotgun, and demanded that he put his hands behind his back. At this point, the suspect lunged at the officer and grabbed the barrel of his shotgun and began trying to pull it out of his hands. The officer held tight and began pulling back. It looked very much like a tug-of-war over the gun. The crowd loved it. They were cheering on this guy and cursing at us.

I was holding my shotgun with my left hand on the pump and my right hand on the wooden stock. When I saw that this guy could potentially wrest the gun from my fellow officer, I moved in to assist. As hard as I could, I thrust the wooden gunstock of my shotgun directly into the guy's forehead. He went down like a rock, with blood flowing from a gash that went from his nose to his hairline. I then stood over him as another officer attempted to place cuffs on him. The other three officers and I stood in a circle and just pointed our guns outward, scanning back and forth in front of the crowd that was now raging.

Before my partner could get the cuffs on the suspect, he came to and began fighting again. Since I was the one standing directly over him, he grabbed me around both of my legs in an attempt to tackle me to the ground. I raised my shotgun in the air and brought the butt of the gun violently down, striking him in the back of his head. I hit him three or four times before he released me and went unconscious. We dragged him from the scene, keeping our guns pointed toward the crowd in case someone felt the need to come and rescue their friend. We got out of there as quickly as we could.

Anyone who spends a career in law enforcement will inevitably (and unfortunately) see danger and death up close and personal. My friend Mary McCord was a young police detective working undercover making "street buys" in an area of the city known for illegal drug activity. I had only been on the street for a few months when a call went out over the radio that a police officer had been shot. Any cop will tell you that listening to radio traffic where another officer is in trouble is the most gut-wrenching thing you can experience, especially if you are not in a position to render aid, but instead can only monitor the traffic and hope against hope that someone will get there in time before disaster occurs.

It truly is a helpless feeling when you know that one of your fellow officers is in trouble and there's nothing you can do to help. It is an inescapable feeling to know that it just as easily could be you who is in need of assistance. We all know that every time you put on that uniform, every time you answer a call, every time you make an arrest, someone might try to kill you. Mary had just made an undercover buy from a drug dealer, and when she identified herself as a police officer and told him he was under arrest, he pulled out a gun and shot her to death. She bled out and died in the middle of the street.

Nothing I've experienced is more sobering than a police funeral. Over a thousand people attended her funeral. Police agencies from all over the state of Alabama sent officers to attend. The funeral procession down I-85 in Montgomery was several miles long. There were big, burly police officers, real "he-men," crying like babies. Everyone in attendance that day must have had a surreal feeling and realization that next time, "It might be me."

J. R. Ward was a good friend and an exceptional police officer. We played softball together on the MPD softball team and worked the streets together on many occasions. A couple of years after I left the police department, I heard about what happened to my friend. How he was out one night and got into a foot pursuit of a suspect for some low-level crime. The guy ran behind a building to hide and when J. R. followed, the scum stepped out with a gun and shot and killed him. Later that year I sat with his widow on the lawn of the US Capitol in Washington, DC, at the annual police memorial held every May in our nation's capital (by that time I was working at US Customs Headquarters there).

At times like this, every law enforcement officer is keenly aware of the adage, "But for the grace of God, there go I." Ironically, J. R.'s murder happened in one of Montgomery's low-income housing projects that I had patrolled many, many times years earlier. I still remember driving through there so many times during the day and stopping my patrol car. Kids from all over would come to the car and I would let them play with the PA mike or the blue lights. Sometimes I would have a bag of candy that I would pass out. I just wanted them to know that cops were not the bad guys. I can't help but wonder if one of those kids grew up to be the one that killed J. R.

Most people that make a career in law enforcement do it because they are "called" to do so. The pay is not that great and the risk is immeasurable, but we do it out of a sense of duty to our fellow man and our community. Most people that go into the field because they think it seems like a really good job don't usually last. To have a long and successful career in any field (but especially law enforcement), you need to be passionate about it. I had that passion. For me, this was a "calling."

My first true mentor in law enforcement was a longtime Montgomery cop by the name of Grady Arnette. He started his career in the '50s and saw quite a lot as the South went through the transformative and tumultuous civil rights era of the '60s and '70s. Major Grady was there when the South was blowing up with riots, civil rights marches, and the Klan. He was there when Martin Luther King Jr. and Hank Williams Sr. were arrested and placed in the Montgomery city jail. He was, above all else, a man of incredible character and honesty. He showed me what being a cop was all about.

Our chief back then was also an old-timer who came up through the ranks with Major Grady. His name was Charles Swindall. Chief Swindall gave me a piece of advice once that became indelibly etched into my soul. He told me, "David, if you stay around this job long enough, you're going to realize that there are lots of people out there that just plain need protecting."

What he meant was twofold. There would certainly be some who are feeble and weak and not able to adequately protect themselves from those who would do them harm. But there were also going to be those too stupid to realize and/or acknowledge that evil exists in this world and that a law enforcement officer with a gun might be the only thing between an innocent person and destruction.

So many bleeding-heart liberals out there will never acknowledge this fact. They excuse the evildoer because they "didn't grow up in the right environment" or "they were spanked or abused as a child" or that their socioeconomic condition "caused" them to pursue a life of crime. All total crap! These people refuse to call evil *evil*, and look at the police as the problem and not the solution. They think that if we just try to "understand" these miscreants and not lock them up, we will be able to talk them out of their aberrant behavior and make everything fine. I have a name for these people: morons.

Besides the weak and helpless, these are the people Chief Swindall was talking about. He knew that in spite of their misguided sentiments toward those that commit crimes, a criminal would not hesitate to take their stuff or cause them bodily harm if given the chance. The chief was letting me know that our obligations included doing everything we could to protect them as well, even though they would never admit to needing protection. Many of these people would always look upon me in my uniform as the culprit and not their friend. Of course, that is until they were robbed or assaulted.

There are, and always will be, naysayers out there who only complain about police officers. How cops are nothing but a bunch of power-hungry people who want nothing more than to harass innocent people for their own self-aggrandizement. Now that's not to say that police abuse and corruption doesn't exist. It certainly does and always will. But those cases are the exception rather than the rule.

Some cops develop what we called the "John Wayne Syndrome." This is when a person gets his or her badge and gun (and the authority that comes with them) and misuses that authority in a domineering way over regular people. They feel a need to display how tough they are and how they are "bigger and badder than you."

I have always felt that it is a privilege to carry a gun and badge. I truly feel that the authority that comes with the position should never be used to intimidate or demean the people that an officer encounters. To be sure, it is sometimes necessary and appropriate to use all of one's power, as well as that of your fellow officers, to quell a disturbance or make an arrest. Making a traffic stop or an arrest for a nonviolent offense can and should be done with a certain degree of respect shown to the subject being detained. People absolutely deserve to be shown respect up until the point they forfeit that right by their own behavior.

For every instance of police corruption or abuse highlighted by the media, there are thousands, if not tens of thousands, of instances not reported of police officers helping people, of police officers saving lives or protecting people and property. To be sure, the idiots who complain most about who we are and what we do would be the last ones who would want to live in a place where the police are absent. These people hate cops . . . that is, until they need one.

My patrol shift on Easter Sunday, 1982, began quietly. My partner and I were on "routine" patrol when we heard the radio operator call a motorcycle unit. The motorman, Steve Coker, had stopped a driver several minutes before and had written him a ticket for a traffic violation. As was standard procedure, he ran a "wants and warrants" check on the driver. For whatever reason, the radio operator did not respond with the results of the check in a timely manner, so Steve let the driver go. The radio operator was now calling Steve to tell him that the check was in. It indicated that the subject had multiple outstanding warrants, all misdemeanors. Steve now needed to go find him to lock him up on the warrants. He asked the radio operator for his home address. She responded with the address that just happened to be in our district. I picked up the radio mike and made the notification that we would be in route to the address to meet the motor unit and assist in the apprehension and arrest. As soon as we pulled into the driveway in front of the house, we heard a shot ring out.

"Two-eleven, shots fired, need assistance," I shouted into the mike as my partner and I exited our patrol car.

Steve was standing on the front porch near the front door. "He just fired at me and ran out the back door," he shouted as he backed away from the door.

Not knowing which way he ran once out the back door, I ran down the sidewalk in one direction and my partner went the other. Two houses down I noticed an opening between the houses and made my way in that direction, hoping to cut him off if he indeed was running that way to make his escape. This was a very old part of Montgomery and the houses were pretty much dilapidated. They were all wood-frame houses that sat up on blocks about three feet off the ground to allow the air to move underneath them. This was to help keep them from getting too hot in the summer months. The only air-conditioning units in this part of town would have been window units, if anyone on this block could have afforded them. Most could not.

As I reached the front-right corner of one house, the subject suddenly appeared at the rear corner and, upon seeing me, immediately raised the rifle he was carrying in my direction. I dove back behind the front of the house for cover. Since the house was elevated on cinder blocks, I was able to see him by looking under the house toward the backyard.

"Police, drop the weapon!" I yelled as loudly as I could.

The other officers on the scene had taken chase and were closing in on the suspect from the other direction. He was pinned in with no place to go. He turned his rifle and fired another shot at the officers behind him. The rifle round struck a wooden outbuilding less than a foot from Detective Bob Davis's head, who had arrived on the scene to assist moments after we did. The bullet exploded in the wood-frame building, shooting splinters into Bob's cheek and forehead.

Still lying on the ground in the front yard and able to clearly see him by looking under the house, I came up on one knee and took aim at him. I fired my shot at about the same time that Bob and Steve had gotten in range and also began firing. Several shots rang out in rapid succession and I saw the suspect fall to the ground. I got up and ran around to the back where he had fallen.

The first thing I saw was Bob kicking and stomping on the guy's face and head, shouting, "You almost shot me, you son of a bitch!"

Near-death encounters like this produce an adrenaline rush that is inexplicable unless you've experienced it for yourself. Individuals react differently when under this level of stress. While Bob's reaction may not have been necessarily appropriate, it was certainly understandable.

Steve and I grabbed Bob and pulled him away to try and calm him down. I then reached down and placed handcuffs on the suspect, who was lying facedown in the dirt and was still alive. By this time there were several other units arriving on the scene, and one immediately called for the paramedics.

Every cop on duty at that moment would have been anxiously listening to the radio, wanting to know if all the cops were safe. I radioed in that the suspect was in custody, that he had been shot, and that all officers were okay. As we waited on the paramedics to arrive, I distinctly remember seeing dirt fly in front of the subject's face each time he exhaled. Moments later we could all hear his breathing become more labored and then suddenly stop. I leaned in closer and could see that the dirt in front of his face was no longer being disturbed. He had expired.

I reached for my handheld radio.

"Two-eleven," I said into my walkie-talkie.

"Two-eleven, go," came the response.

"You can have the paramedics slow down," I said. "Subject is code thirteen."

Cop work in general is full of "routine," or noneventful occurrences, with moments of high stress and adrenaline rushes sprinkled in. It's difficult to fully understand or adequately explain what a cop goes through in his or her job. Because of this, cops mostly hang out with other cops when off duty. One of the "releases" most popular with my fellow officers and me was something we called "choir practice." This was a term that had been coined by famed police author Joseph Wambaugh. Basically, choir practice took place anytime police officers got together to drink. We used to hold our choir practice at Hank's grave.

Legendary country star Hank Williams Sr.'s grave is located in Oakwood Cemetery, which is directly next door to police head-quarters in downtown Montgomery. His gravesite is a beautiful, large, marble memorial, including a big marble cast of his hat. Since drinking in uniform was against police regulations, cops would simply remove their shirts and sit on Hank's grave in their undershirts and drink away the stressors of the job. Of course, you weren't supposed to transport your personal booze in a city vehicle, or for that matter operate a city vehicle after drinking either.

Those regulations were somehow overlooked because it was just too much trouble to go all the way home, change clothes, and then drive your personal car back to Hank's—especially since he was right next door when you got off shift! I can even remember one Saturday afternoon seeing a motorcycle cop friend of mine drive by on his bike. His saddlebag in the back (a compartment used to store a ticket book, windbreaker, and so forth) was leaking water and leaving a stream on the asphalt behind him as he rode by. Because I knew him well, I knew that he was using his saddlebag as a cooler again and had a full supply of iced-down beer with him.

After a year of working the streets in a patrol car, I thought it would be great to become a motorman. They just looked so cool. This was during the heyday of the TV police show *Chips*. The high leather boots with your pants legs tucked in, cruising the streets on your own without a partner was very appealing. There was always the danger of "laying" your bike down, but I figured the risk was worth the reward. The first rule of being a motorman was not if you would ever go down, but when and how bad.

One of the most dangerous assignments for motormen was working a funeral escort. A team of motormen would lead a funeral procession from a church or funeral home and escort the procession to the cemetery. In order to keep the procession intact all the way to the gravesite, it would be necessary for us to leapfrog each other from intersection to intersection in order to get to the next intersection before the lead vehicle (usually the hearse) arrived. We wanted to have the traffic stopped so that the line of cars could proceed without stopping. As one motorman held up traffic at an intersection, he would wait for the last car in line to pass and then jump on his bike and race ahead, leapfrogging the next motorman and beat the procession line to the next intersection. This required us to travel at seventy or eighty miles per hour, within a couple feet of the line of cars all the way to the front of the line. I was always amazed that none of us ever went down doing this.

Riding a motor meant you were by yourself most of the time and didn't have a partner right there with you if you got into trouble and needed immediate help. Other units were always close by, but usually took at least a couple of minutes to respond to your location if you called out for help over the radio. I once pulled over a car for an expired tag in a "not-so-good" part of town. I called in the location of the stop and the car's tag number (standard procedure) and then got off my bike and approached the driver. The first thing I noticed when I reached the driver-side door was the size of the guy behind the wheel. He was massive. As I was looking over his driver's license, dispatch radioed back to inform me that the car's tag came back to an individual with several outstanding arrest warrants for unpaid traffic tickets.

I knew right then that I was going to have to place him under arrest and that I would need a patrol car to come and provide transport. I requested a unit to assist. I then asked the driver to exit his vehicle. My heart began to race as the guy stepped out from behind the wheel. He was about 6'5" and had to weigh at least 350 pounds. His hands looked like catcher's mitts and his arms and wrists were about the size of my legs. It crossed my mind very quickly that if this guy resisted arrest in any way, I was going to be in trouble. The patrol unit coming to assist me could not get there fast enough, I thought.

"Do you know that you have a bunch of unpaid tickets?" I asked him.

"Yes," he replied.

"You know that means I have to arrest you," I said.

"Yeah, I kinda figured that," he said.

I had stepped back away from him a few feet, just outside of arm's length, for my safety. Up to this point he had been completely calm and had not given me any problems, but I knew that could change at any second.

"I'm going to be perfectly honest with you," I began. "As big as you are, if you try to resist in any way, I will have no choice but to shoot you," I said as I placed my hand on my pistol still in my holster.

"Don't worry," he said. "I ain't gonna give you no trouble."

Believe me when I tell you how glad I was to hear him say that. About this time the patrol unit rolled up and two more cops got out and came over. A giant sense of relief washed over me. I removed my handcuffs from my belt and asked the guy to put his hands behind him. He immediately complied. When I attempted to place my cuffs on his wrists, I saw something I have never seen before or since. His wrists were so big the cuffs would not fit over them (picture trying to put handcuffs over your calf or thigh).

"Holy shit," said one of the other officers. "This guy's huge!"

Thankfully, the guy just sort of chuckled. He was indeed a gentle giant. We ended up having to use three sets of cuffs to properly secure him. I looped my cuffs around one wrist, much like putting on a bracelet, and then did the same on the other wrist. I then used the third set of handcuffs to secure together the two cuffs now on both of his wrists, and we transported him to jail without incident.

My only serious wreck happened one Saturday afternoon in front of the Sears on Fairview Avenue in Montgomery. I was cruising at about forty miles per hour as I approached an intersection.

There was a panel truck in the lane to my left waiting to make a left turn when oncoming traffic cleared. Across from this van in the opposite direction was a car waiting to make a left hand turn into the Sears parking lot. This car could not see me making my way down the right hand lane because their view was blocked by the van. The lady driving the car decided to go ahead and make her turn and crossed directly in my path as I came alongside the van.

She appeared so quickly in front of me that I did not even have time to apply my brakes and attempt to avoid a collision. At forty miles per hour I T-boned her in the passenger-side door of her car. The impact catapulted me off my bike and shot me over her car. My helmet hit the top of her car as I went over her, doing a front flip. I landed on the street, feet first, right next to her driver-side door. I hit the ground and rolled over two or three times before coming to rest.

She immediately opened her door and began crying and screaming, "I'm so sorry, I'm so sorry. Are you okay?"

People in the Sears parking lot ran over to get a closer look. I remember hearing someone yell, "Did you see that policeman fly over that car?"

Other than some scratches from the pavement and a slight limp, I was relatively unscathed. I can't say the same for my bike, though. I walked back around her car to assess the damage to my bike and to use the radio to call it in. My beloved motorcycle looked like an accordion. The tires were touching each other underneath a cracked engine block. Oil was gushing out onto the street. I picked up the radio mike.

"Forty-six—I'm down. Sears on Fairview."

Within minutes I began hearing the sounds of sirens as other units came to check on me, in addition to the paramedics being dispatched. I was transported to the ER for a precautionary check, but was released shortly thereafter.

A few weeks later I was back on duty with another bike and was assigned to work traffic at an Alabama concert due to take place at the Montgomery Civic Center. Motormen were always utilized to work the traffic in and around these venues whenever an event was taking place. We would always find a place in front of the building to park our bikes, usually up on a curb or sidewalk, and then dismount and walk to our assigned post. Several other motormen were already there, and a long line of patrons was lining up, waiting to go inside for the concert. I slowly pulled my bike up over the curb in front of the civic center, intending to park it next to the other bikes already there.

I was barely moving as I approached my parking spot when I lost my balance and felt the bike going over. I fell sideways and the weight of the bike landed on my leg. All of this happened right in front of the other motormen, as well as the crowd of people waiting to attend the concert. My fellow officers all burst out laughing. Many in line thought it was pretty funny as well. I was so embarrassed that somehow I was able to quickly push the bike off my leg and stand it up on the kickstand. No doubt the adrenaline rush from the embarrassment gave me the strength necessary to pick up a five-hundred-pound bike!

U.S. CUSTOMS
THE DEPARTMENT OF THE
TREASURY
THE DEPARTMENT OF THE TREASURY
1789
SPECIAL AGENT
27638

III. US CUSTOMS AND JOINING THE WAR ON DRUGS

ALMOST FIVE YEARS INTO MY CAREER WITH THE MONTGOMERY PD, I decided to accept a job offer with the US Customs Service. I had been trying to get on with the feds for over a year with no success. I first applied to be an FBI agent and took the entrance exam at the local FBI office in Montgomery. I knew the FBI resident agent-in-charge from my tenure as an instructor at the Montgomery Police Academy. He was a frequent guest instructor. When I showed up to take the test, he took me to the side and, because of our friendship, quietly told me that I had virtually no chance at getting hired.

"David, I think you'd make a great agent, but you have a big problem," he said. "You're a white male, and the Bureau is only hiring blacks and women."

My first real introduction into how the federal workplace operates. I would see very little change over the next twenty-eight years!

I subsequently took the treasury enforcement agent exam because I was interested in becoming an agent with the ATF. The only problem was they weren't hiring at this time. Instead, I received a call from a marine enforcement supervisor with US Customs. I knew nothing about US Customs. They weren't even on my radar.

But I figured, "Hey, why not? It's federal."

They were doing a mass hiring in response to the War on Drugs that the Reagan administration was engaged in, and they were creating a large marine enforcement force to help combat the drugs being smuggled by boats into South Florida. I resigned from the Montgomery PD in April 1986, and immediately reported for US Customs training at FLETC. Following a sixteen-week academy, I reported for duty in the Miami office.

It didn't take long for me to think I had died and gone to heaven. I reported for duty each day wearing shorts, boat shoes, and usually a T-shirt. We would sometimes wear a uniform if we worked the day shift and especially if we conducted our marine patrols on a marked vessel like the *Blue Thunder* boat. But initially I worked the midnight shift, and that was always on an unmarked boat. The supervision was limited as well. Once we pulled away from the dock at Papa-100 (our marine base located on the Miami River), we were on our own to go where we wanted and do whatever we felt like. Many times the seas would be rough and nobody wanted to take the boat "outside" in bad weather or rough sea conditions. There were hundreds of little canals all around Biscayne Bay and many small docks where we could happen upon a smuggler. Bad weather days were usually spent patrolling these areas.

One time after reporting for duty on the midnight shift, my partner and I decided to take an unmarked car out and "check the docks." The weather was really bad and taking a boat out would have been miserable. We headed out down the Venetian Causeway when we pulled alongside a car with two teenagers in it. The kid in the passenger seat looked over at us and started waving around what looked like a marijuana joint. He was laughing while he did it, obviously having no clue as to who we were.

I just smiled back at him and then looked over at my partner and said, "Now this is gonna be fun."

I slowed down a bit and let him pass by me and then pulled in behind him as we continued down the road. I then pulled a blue light from the floor of our car, set it on the dash, and then plugged it in. The driver immediately pulled over.

My partner and I got out and approached their car. We were wearing plainclothes, so I took my badge out and identified ourselves as federal agents. The kid in the passenger seat who had been waving the joint and laughing at us had a whole new attitude. I asked both kids to get out of the car and step to the side so we could talk.

"Whose car is this?" I asked.

The driver told me it belonged to his dad.

"Does your dad know that you're driving around town smoking grass in his car?" I asked.

The driver looked over at his friend, obviously pissed at him.

"Do you think your dad is going to be happy when he has to come bail you two out of jail and pick his car up at the impound lot?" I asked.

The driver just looked down in obvious distress and buried his head in his hands.

"Oh, God," he said. "He's gonna kill me."

"Tell you what," I said. "If there's no pot, then I don't have any reason to arrest you two, now do I?"

Both kids looked at me with a quizzical look on their faces.

"I'm not going to let you throw it away because you'll just come back and pick it up after we're gone," I said. "But if your friend ate all the evidence, then we would have no reason to lock you up, now would we?"

The driver got the hint. He looked over at his friend and started shouting at him, "Eat it, eat it!"

His friend reached in the car and grabbed the joint he had already lit and a small baggie of pot and started shoving it all in his mouth. After a couple minutes of doing this, the guy started coughing and then began throwing up all over the side of his friend's car.

I looked at the driver and said, "Well, I guess you're free to go."

He thanked me profusely, and we got back in our car and drove away.

I worked with some real characters in the boat division those first couple of years with Customs. Our supervisor was a great guy named Joe Goulet. We called him "Turbo Joe" because he was always firing on all cylinders and was NEVER in need of a caffeine jolt like the rest of us. Joe Peters was one of the guys on our crew. J. P. was a guy that did not spend a lot of time worrying about his personal physical fitness. He was about 5'8" and weighed somewhere north of 300 pounds. Turbo Joe nicknamed J. P. "The QTR." This moniker came from a story in the local paper about some 450-pound guy that was on trial for rape. The paper had dubbed him "The Quarter-Ton Rapist." Joe thought the nickname worked and we all thought it was hilarious.

The QTR was famous for always falling asleep on the boat. He could be dead asleep and if someone walked up with a piping-hot pizza or a bag of warm burgers, he would immediately come awake, looking for the source of the aroma that had awakened him from his slumber. He was more than happy to help devour whatever food someone else had brought onboard.

We mostly just rode around enjoying the fact that we were getting paid to drive around a high-performance speedboat. One particular night that we were on patrol, my crew decided to get a late-night snack at a Wendy's restaurant we knew stayed open all night. As we idled down a canal that led to a dock near this Wendy's, we noticed that another Customs boat on duty that night had the same idea that we did. As we got closer to the dock, I noticed their boat was not sitting level in the water. It was leaning almost forty-five degrees. When we got right next to them we immediately figured out why.

That other Customs crew had gone there to eat and, after finishing their meal, had all sacked out on the boat. While they all slept, the tide had gone out, causing the water level to lower dramatically. Since they had secured their boat to a pair of cleats on the dock, the boat was literally hanging off the cleats, barely touching the water. After they awoke at hearing us approach, they had to use a knife to cut the lines in order to free themselves from the dock.

"Don't worry," I told the other boat captain. "We won't tell anybody."

Of course I was lying. We couldn't wait to get back to the office and tell the other guys. Everybody had a good laugh at their expense.

The TV show *Miami Vice* was big during this time. We used to see them filming scenes quite frequently. Unlike the show, encountering smugglers and chasing them down was not a nightly, weekly, or even monthly occurrence. Most shifts were uneventful.

Sometimes we made seizures with no effort at all. About three a.m. one night we came in contact with a boat that had obviously run aground in Biscayne Bay. On board were about thirty large duffel bags filled with bricks of cocaine. The idiot smugglers had not looked at their charts and were unaware they were headed for a sandbar on their way to wherever their drop-off point was. Once aground, they simply abandoned their load and swam away. Besides the cocaine, we were able to seize their boat, which was a beautiful and sleek go-fast with two outboard 350-horsepower engines. This boat would soon join the War on Drugs as an asset for us.

In the early days of my Customs career, I genuinely thought that this job I had stumbled into was simply too good to be true. It certainly could be dangerous at times, but it mostly was a lot of fun.

In 1987 I went with a marine enforcement team from Miami to the Virgin Islands for a three-week TDY (temporary duty). Our assignment was to turn over to the Virgin Islands police two go-fast boats that had been seized by the Customs office in San Juan. After turning over the boats, our duties would shift to providing them the necessary training for them to properly operate these high-performance watercrafts. Our team flew from the Virgin Islands to San Juan, where we picked up the two boats and then drove them from San Juan over to the Virgin Islands. Each morning for the next three weeks, we would meet a group of Virgin Islands police at the dock in Charlotte Amalie, gas up and preflight the boats, and then spend the entire day just tooling around the waters of the Virgin Islands. The weather was always sublime and since the boats were unmarked, we usually went shirtless all day, working on our tans. The Virgin Islands have a beautiful harbor area with lots of tourists and lots of boats. I remember a large pontoon boat that served as a floating bar that moved mostly tourists around the harbor. A couple of times a day we would pull up alongside this floating bar and order a few slushy drinks and then continue on with our "patrol" and "training." It was hard to believe we were getting paid for this!

This same year, US Customs began an ongoing operation in coordination with the Bahamian Defense Force (BDF). Since we knew that many smuggling ventures into South Florida began with boats picking up loads in Bahamian waters, we wanted to attack the problem by going to the source. We wanted to catch them over there first, before they made their way across the Atlantic. Since we had no jurisdiction in Bahamian waters, we had to have a BDF officer onboard if we were to engage in any type of enforcement activities within the boundaries of the Bahama Islands. This initiative became known as Operation Cat Cay.

Cat Cay is a small island in the Bahamian chain due east from Miami, approximately forty-five miles away. Cat Cay was developed as an island getaway for the rich and powerful. Bebe Rebozo, close friend of former president Nixon, had a home there. Although I missed him by one day once, Nixon came over for a visit during one of our operations there. Another frequent visitor to the island was Bernie Little, a huge name in the world of offshore boat racing. Bernie was a close friend of the Busch family (of Anheuser-Busch beer).

Augie Busch III, chairman and CEO of Anheuser Busch at that time, was staying on Bernie's boat during one of my many two-week deployments for Operation Cat Cay. A sixty-foot Hatteras yacht was kept docked in the Cat Cay marina and used as the "base station" for our Cat Cay operation. One Sunday afternoon I was sitting in the Hatteras, waiting for a new three-man crew heading over from Miami to begin their two-week duty tour, when I noticed a couple of workers unloading several cases of beer from the back of Bernie Little's yacht. One guy was handing down a case at a time and the other guy was stacking them on a handcart. When the stack reached his chin, he began rolling his handcart down the dock and over in our direction. When he reached our boat, I stepped outside to greet him. "Compliments from Mr. Busch," he said. I looked across the marina and there was Mr. Busch standing on the back of Bernie's yacht, waving at me and giving a "thumbs-up" sign. All of the Cat Cay residents and visitors knew who we were and why we were there. They were all supportive of our efforts and were always very friendly.

There was a nine-hole golf course on the island, as well. Many of us always took our golf clubs with us and would play the course during the day (most of the operations would take place at night). One day I was playing golf by myself and came upon an elderly gentleman playing in front of me. He asked me to join him for the next few holes, which I did. He knew right away that I was one of the Customs agents and told me how glad he was that we were trying to do something about all the smuggling that was being originated out of the Bahamas. He introduced himself as Willard Rockwell Jr. Many years earlier, Mr. Rockwell had taken over his father's company and turned it into Rockwell International, a huge conglomerate that had been heavily involved in the defense and aerospace industries. He had recently retired, he told me, and spent most of his time at his house on Cat Cay.

Besides an occasional round of golf, we always made sure we brought dive tanks with us on the boat to give us something else to do during our down time. There were lots of lobsters swimming around the waters of Cat Cay, and we made concerted efforts to catch as many as we could. One time we made a lobster haul with very little effort. We boarded a Bahamian lobster boat and the first thing I noticed when we got onboard were the three fifty-five-gallon drums filled to the top with bugs (what the Bahamians called lobsters). As soon as the boat captain saw our BDF officer, he immediately took out his ruler and began measuring the lobsters one at a time, making sure they were the required length for harvesting according to Bahamian regulations. Whenever he pulled one out that was too small, he threw it over the side. He did this several times before I finally suggested to him that instead of throwing the small ones out, he should just toss them in the empty bucket that was sitting next to his chair, and that I would make sure they were returned to the water. He smiled back at me and immediately began filling up the bucket. The bugs never made it back to the water. Instead, they ended up on our grill that evening covered with butter and consumed by our crew.

Just north of Cat Cay is the island of Bimini, which had been overrun by smugglers. While the people we encountered on Cat Cay liked and supported us, those on Bimini were completely the opposite. Prior to the ramping up of Operation Cat Cay, smugglers spent a lot of time (and a lot of money) on Bimini. They had lots of cash to throw around and the locals on Bimini were happy to be the recipients. Our presence in and around Bimini eventually drove the smugglers away, and they took their cash with them. The locals hated us for that.

One night while on patrol, we pulled up to an almost empty dock to just take a rest for a while. The dockmaster saw us and made his way out to meet us. He was screaming at us the whole way up the dock.

"I don't think this guy wants us here," I said to my crewmates.

Our BDF officer with us that night was a guy named Juan. He quietly sat there and said nothing as this dockmaster cussed at us and told us to get the hell off his dock. He then looked at Juan and began berating him for associating himself with us and questioning his Bahamian allegiance. Juan had had enough.

BDF officers carried Sten guns, which were WWII-era British submachine guns. Juan carried his on a shoulder strap. He stepped up on the dock from our boat, pulled back the slide on his Sten gun, and racked in a live round. He then placed the tip of the barrel on top of the dockmaster's head, just above his forehead. All of a sudden Juan pulled the trigger and fired off a quick three-round burst. With the barrel now smoking hot, he thrust the muzzle into the guy's Adam's apple and demanded that he leave us alone and get off his dock. He left us immediately, no doubt in need of a new pair of shorts! We never had a problem with that guy again.

Negotiating the waters between Cat Cay and Bimini (a distance of about fifteen miles) could be hazardous due to the large rock outcroppings sticking out of the water. This was no problem during daylight hours, especially if the conditions were calm. It was potentially challenging, however, after the sun went down and especially if the seas were rough. There's no ambient light to help you see, like you would get if you were travelling along the Miami coast with all of the light emanating from the buildings along the shoreline. Many a night I drove up and down this path, using our spotlight to illuminate the rocks that could rip apart the bottom of a fiberglass boat if we were so careless as to not see them in the pitch blackness of a Bahamian night. Unfortunately, this happened to another boat crew during one of my Cat Cay operation deployments.

Larry Sanders was a fellow boat captain out of the Ft. Lauderdale office getting ready to deploy one night out of our Cat Cay base.

"The seas are rough, Larry," I told him as he and his crew were about to depart. "Be careful."

Larry told me his intentions were to head for Bimini and find some nice, quiet dock. All he wanted to do was sit out the storm that had been brewing most of the day. My crew had just come back in from our shift, and I knew how rough it really was out there.

"Good idea," I told him in response to his stated plans for the night.

Early the next morning we began receiving calls on our base station radio from Coast Guard Miami, telling us that one of our Cat Cay crews had been sending out distress signals and that they were in need of rescue. Since Larry's crew was the only crew out at that time, I knew it had to be them. We loaded up our boat and immediately headed out of Cat Cay for Bimini. Several hundred yards from Bimini, we saw a very disturbing sight. A Customs intercept boat atop a large rock sticking out of the water, with waves from the heavy seas crashing around it. I pulled our boat close enough to allow one of my crewmembers to disembark and climb up on the rock. He looked inside their boat and hollered back to us that no one was inside. Since they had been able to radio their distress, I felt confident that Larry and his crew were safe, but where the heck were they?

We began calling for them on the radio but could get no response. We pulled up to the first dock we found in the Bimini harbor and got out and started walking back toward Larry's boat. About this time Larry and his two crewmembers exited a parked car near where we had docked and made their way toward us.

"Larry," I said, "are you guys okay?"

Other than being drenched, disheveled, and cold, they seemed to be all right.

"I've been trying to raise you on the radio," I said. "Why didn't you answer?"

"Our walkie-talkie batteries died a couple hours ago," he said, which explained why we hadn't heard from him.

What happened to them the night before was a stark illustration of how dangerous this job could be. As Larry was negotiating his vessel between the rocks that help make up the Bahamian island chain, they somehow missed seeing the giant rock that they eventually hit. Fortunately for them, the tide had been up at the time they wrecked. This allowed them to "land" on top of the rock where it was relatively flat, instead of striking the side of it head on, which is what would have happened if it had been low tide.

There was a walking path from where we were all the way to the stranded boat, as long as you could keep your balance on all of the rocks. I suggested we go and check out the boat. Every time we took a boat out on patrol for the Cat Cay operation, we took along an AR-15 assault rifle.

"Where's your AR?" I asked.

"Still on the boat," he replied.

"Uh-oh," I said. "I hope it's still there."

When we made it to the boat, I climbed aboard and opened the hatch to the forward cabin area where I knew the AR-15 was normally stored. In addition to the normal equipment that comes with a high-performance boat of this kind, our Customs boats were also equipped with a very high-tech and expensive satellite radio, worth tens of thousands of US taxpayer dollars.

"Oh, God," was all I could say when I looked inside.

Apparently, during the night some locals from Bimini had broken the lock to the hatch door and rummaged around inside, looking for anything of value they could steal. The AR-15 was gone, of course, but the thieves must have wanted us to know that they had been there. Before leaving, they used OUR assault rifle to pepper the inside of the cabin with dozens of rounds, obliterating the satellite radio!

When my two children were small, their favorite bedtime story was the one I told of the time I fell into the water while on patrol one night in the Bahamas. It was around midnight and our crew happened upon a single small boat anchored on the lee side of a large rock island. There was no doubt they were waiting on an airdrop, but unfortunately we got there before it had occurred. We decided to go ahead and conduct a boarding anyway. J. R. Long was our boat captain that night and at the helm of our boat. He maneuvered in close so that I could jump from our boat to theirs and check their IDs and do a search of their boat. The seas were really rough, and both boats were bouncing around quite a bit. Our Customs boat was bigger and taller, so it was fairly easy to jump from our boat to theirs. After talking with them (they said they were just out there doing some fishing . . . yeah, right!), I searched their boat and found nothing (no surprise there). I waved for J. R. to move back in so that I could get back on our boat.

When he got in close, I stood on the edge of the suspect boat and tried to time my jump with the bouncing up and down of our two boats due to the waves. I knew it was not going to be easy because I was now lower than the level of the Customs boat that I was trying to jump to. As soon as I pushed off and got airborne, I knew I was in trouble. One foot landed on the Customs boat just as a wave hit it from underneath, shooting the bow of our boat straight up into the air. I tried reaching for the railing that was attached to the bow but missed it. I shot up into the air and fell into the water between our two boats. As soon as I hit the water I instinctively used my arms to force my body to go deeper down in the water, knowing that the bow of the Customs boat was about to come crashing down just above my head as it continued to bounce up and down due to the surf.

I could hear J. R. rev the engines in reverse for the same reason, trying to avoid landing on top of me. I waited for a few seconds and then slowly ascended back up. When the top of my hat cleared water level, I looked right at the two suspect guys on their boat who were leaning over the side with a look of disbelief on their faces at what they had just seen. I swam a few feet over to the side of their boat and, with water pouring off the bill of my cap, climbed back into their boat to try it again. The second attempt to reboard the Customs boat was successful and we headed straight back to base so I could dry out my gun (which thankfully stayed secure in my holster) and get out of my soaked uniform.

On another Operation Cat Cay deployment, Eddie Wishneff, John Tobin, a BDF officer, and I were on patrol one afternoon when we passed a boat about five miles west of Bimini, seemingly headed for Florida. We pulled up alongside and signaled for the boat to stop. After tying our boat to theirs, John and I stepped across in order to conduct a typical boarding. We checked their IDs, asked a few standard questions, and then began a cursory search of their boat. Nothing appeared out of order at first glance, but then I noticed that there were no panels to gain access to the area beneath the deck of the boat.

This was a center-console, "open-fisherman"-type vessel. All boats are made with these access panels, and it was certainly odd that they were missing. There was also a faint smell of lacquer, indicating that work had recently been done on the deck. We then immediately escorted them back to Bimini. After tying up, we told them to wait on the dock while we did a more thorough search. John, Eddie, and I then got some pry bars from our boat and began to pry up the deck boards of their boat. As we began this process, the two guys (both Americans) became very uneasy and were obviously worried. As it turned out, they were worried for good reason.

When the first board came up we could immediately see why. There was almost a thousand pounds of marijuana secreted below the deck. We immediately placed the two guys under arrest. A large crowd of people had gathered by now and watched with great interest as we began removing the bales and placing them on the dock. To add insult to injury, we made the two smugglers pose for pictures with us as we snapped some shots of us sitting atop the seized bales. This was the first seizure ever made by American law enforcement in Bahamian territory in a joint US-Bahamas operation. The Customs bosses in Miami and Washington were ecstatic.

While riding boats certainly provided me with more than my share of fun, it also was without a doubt the most dangerous thing I've ever done related to my career. There were always inherent risks that accompanied the job. Being out on the high seas when it was calm was glorious, but it could be treacherous when seas were rough. Once while crossing the Atlantic on our way over to Cat Cay, we hit fifteen- to seventeen-foot waves in the Gulf Stream. The Gulf Stream is a powerful and warm current that runs through the Atlantic and is always more rough than any of the waters off the coasts of either the US or the Bahamas. We probably should have never made the trip. We knew it was going to be a rough ride, but my crew and I decided to make the trip because we knew we would lose the Sunday premium pay, as well as that day's per diem if we waited to go the following day. I must admit that it was pretty stupid in hindsight.

Each time we settled into a trough between the waves, a fifteen-foot-high wall of water would break over the top of us. I truly thought we might not make it. At one point, we came down the backside of one these waves straight down into a trough. The water broke over the front of the boat with such force that the wave actually bent the metal frame around our boat's windshield. The part of the wave that broke above the windshield hit me directly in the face, cracking the face mask on a helmet I was wearing. It ended up taking us almost five hours to make the crossing, which would usually take us about an hour in calm seas.

All boats are equipped with a specific series of lights so that other boats can see them at night. A red light on the starboard bow (front right) and a green light on port bow (front left) help other boats identify which direction you are headed. In other words, if you are on your boat at night and see a red light off in the distance, you know that a boat is there and that it is facing (and/or moving) from your left to right. The opposite is true if you see a green light.

In addition to the red and green lights, large boats are required to have two white lights on poles that extend high above the level of their deck. The aft (rear) light is positioned higher than the forward light. When you are out on the water at night, these lights are sometimes the only things you can see to let you know that a large boat or ship is there. If you look out in the dark and see two white lights, with the higher one on your left and the lower one on your right, then you know which direction the ship is headed (it would be moving from your left to right).

If you can only see one white light, then you know that the ship is moving directly away from you because the forward light would be hidden from your view since it is positioned lower at the front of the ship. Conversely, if you see two white lights, one directly above the other, then you know the ship is headed right toward you. The reason I mention this is because of what almost happened to us one night while on patrol in the Atlantic.

It was about four a.m. and the seas were like glass. We shut off our engines and decided to relax and just drift for a while. Before too long my two crewmates and I had fallen fast asleep. While we dozed, our boat drifted into the middle of the Gulf Stream, which just happened to be the primary shipping lane for the big cargo ships making their way to the Port of Miami.

When I awoke I stood up and began to look around. It was pitch black because of the cloud cover, with no light coming from the moon and stars above. As my vision became clearer, I looked out in the darkness and noticed two white lights, one directly over the other. I immediately realized that I was looking at a large ship that was headed directly toward us.

"Guys, get up," I said. "We better move."

I cranked the engines and began moving out of the path of whatever ship was there. As it turned out, the lights I saw were coming from a giant container ship that was traveling in a direct path toward where we sat. It had gotten to within fifty yards of us when I noticed it and moved our boat out of its path. Had we not moved, the cargo ship would have run over and sank us and, quite likely, never would have known it.

Another close call happened one night after chasing down a smuggler halfway between Miami and Bimini. We had received informant information that an airdrop would be taking place one afternoon. We positioned our boat on the lee side of a giant rock outcropping in the Bahamas and waited. After a while, we spotted an airplane approaching on the horizon and could see the plane through binoculars begin to circle. Shortly thereafter we saw large bundles or bales being dropped from the plane to a waiting boat below. We came out of our hiding place and began racing toward the boat that was picking up the load. They were about four miles away from us when we took off after them. It took about twenty minutes for us to close the gap between our two boats, and as soon as they realized they couldn't get away, they stopped and gave up.

We took them into custody and decided to transport their boat, the prisoners, and some of the bales we retrieved to Miami for processing. I got behind the wheel of the suspect's boat for the trip to Miami. The seas were very calm, and by the time we began our trip the day had turned to night. The suspect boat was a center-console "open-fish" boat with low gunnels (the sides of the boat). The seas were like glass, so I just stood back against the driver's seat, pushed forward the throttle, and settled in for what I thought would be a smooth ride across the Atlantic.

Because it was pitch black, I couldn't see the Customs boat riding along beside me. I had been out front for the first part of this trip and was just cruising along on the calm seas. For some reason, the guy driving the Customs boat decided to pass me and take the lead. When he got out in front of me I was unaware that I was about to hit the wake that his boat was leaving behind him. If I had noticed him passing me, I could have braced myself for his wake and it would have been no problem. Instead, I was used to "riding on glass" thus far and was not prepared for it when his wake crossed in front of me. The front of my boat hit his wake trough and it felt like hitting a brick wall. My boat lunged forward and, when doing so, threw me forward as well. I shot forward and right before going over the side of the boat gunnel, I somehow managed to reach back and grab hold of the railing that surrounded the center console, keeping me from going over the side.

It immediately occurred to me what just almost happened. If I had gone over the side, my boat would have continued on without me because the throttle, when pushed forward, would stay engaged until you actually pulled it back yourself. Since it was so dark, nobody on the Customs boat would have seen me go over the side, and it would have been miles and miles ahead before anyone would have realized that no one was at the helm of the seized boat I was piloting. Meanwhile, I would have been treading water somewhere in the middle of the Atlantic, miles from any coastline. And no, I wasn't wearing a life vest!

Again, pretty stupid in hindsight. In spite of being in two different shooting incidents, a multitude of high-speed chases (both on the water and on the street), and several violent arrests, I consider this the closest to death I've ever come.

Greg Thompson (another marine enforcement officer I frequently worked with) and I took out *Blue Thunder* one day on one of those "Chamber of Commerce" days in Miami. The temperature was about seventy-five degrees, no clouds in the sky, and calm, smooth seas. We were in uniform that day since we were on *Blue Thunder*. As we approached the dock on Cape Florida from the Biscayne Bay side, we could see a lot of activity going on. There were large lights on the tops of poles and lots of people and trucks milling around. We headed that way for a closer look. When we got closer, we could tell that they were shooting some type of movie or TV show. As it turned out, they were filming a movie called *Midnight Crossing* starring Faye Dunaway and Daniel J. Travanti.

When we docked *Blue Thunder*, a few people came over to see what we wanted and probably would have asked us to leave except for the fact that we were in uniform and driving this big boat with "US Customs" emblazoned on the side. Faye Dunaway walked past me and sort of turned her nose up as she went by without saying a word. Then Daniel J. Travanti walked over. I recognized him immediately because I had always been a big fan of *Hill Street Blues*, a TV cop show from the '70s that he starred in. He couldn't have been nicer. He was admiring *Blue Thunder* and asking us about our job, when it occurred to me that he might want to go for a ride. VIP rides, as we called them, on *Blue Thunder* had become very common because the "brass" at Customs was always ready to show off their "signature" weapon in the War on Drugs. Once we cleared it with the Miami office, I asked Travanti if he wanted to go for a ride. His eyes lit up as if he couldn't believe what I was asking him.

"Are you kidding?" he said. "I'd love to."

He and another guy working on the set jumped aboard and off we went. We left the bay and headed out to the ocean. Once we cranked it up to full throttle I looked over at him and I could tell he loved every second of it. When we got about ten miles off shore, I turned *Blue Thunder* around so we could head back to the dock. I then asked Travanti if he wanted to give it a try. Again, he couldn't believe what he was hearing. He stepped in behind the wheel and I gave him a quick lesson on what to do and off we went.

Once he got the boat up on plane, I kept telling him, "More throttle, more throttle."

He was like a kid in a candy store. I think that day turned out to be the highlight for him of making that movie. As best I remember, the movie was a real dud! When we got back to the dock he had a photographer come over and take a picture of him behind the wheel with his arm around my neck. The following week an envelope for me showed up in the mail with the picture inside and his inscription, "Dave, thanks for the ride, Daniel J. Travanti."

I spent about two and half years on boats in the Customs Marine Division and explicitly knew how lucky I was to have such a fun job. Yeah, it could be rough at times and physically demanding, but all in all, getting to ride around in a $300,000 ocean racer was a pretty cool job to have and I always knew it.

We sometimes worked in coordination with the Customs Air Wing when chasing down targets in the Atlantic. One afternoon we responded to a call from BLOC (Blue Lightning Operation Center) that had spotted a target on radar that needed checking out. A Customs Citation aircraft had also been dispatched and was flying overhead while we searched for this suspect boat. It turned out to be nothing, but after riding around for a while I radioed the plane above and thanked them for their assist. Then I thought of something that might be fun. As they began to fly away back to their base in Homestead, Florida, I called the air unit one last time.

"Hey, before you guys go back, how 'bout a little chicken?"

The Customs pilot knew just what I meant. His plane began to bank and turn back toward us. When he was facing us head on, I revved our boat and got to top speed and we raced directly toward each other, similar to the game of "chicken" when two cars race at each other head on and see which car will be the "chicken" and swerve to avoid a head-on collision. As the plane passed over our heads, I got back on the radio and taunted them.

"Are you serious, is that as low as you can go?"

I turned our boat around as he banked another turn and headed for us again. On this pass he dropped his plane to about twenty feet off the ocean's surface and zoomed right over the tops of our heads as we passed underneath.

One of the guys on my crew said, "Now that was cool."

One "not-so-cool" incident happened once when I reported for the midnight shift. My supervisor "Turbo Joe" Goulet informed me that there was a Hollywood screenwriter in town that wanted to go out with us on patrol so he could observe what we did firsthand to help him with a movie he was writing about drug smuggling. It just so happened that on this particular night, the weather was extremely harsh and the seas were very rough. Normally on nights like this we either kept our boat on the "inside" (canals or the bay, not out in the ocean), or we didn't take the boat out at all.

Joe told me, "Just go out a few miles, talk about what you do on a normal patrol, and then come back. You should be fine."

Boy, he could not have been more wrong.

Before we left Papa-100, I told this screenwriter that the seas were up and the ride going out was going to be extremely rough. I showed him how to stand behind my seat and to hang on to the seat railing for support. Most importantly, I told him, was to keep his knees bent as we would be encountering "head" seas (high waves coming at us as we progressed out to sea) and that the boat was going to bounce up and down quite a bit due to the conditions. Keeping his knees bent would allow him to cushion the impact each time the boat bounced off the waves and avoid injuring his legs. Everything seemed to be fine for the first thirty minutes or so as we made our way out of Government Cut, heading due east away from Miami.

Maneuvering a boat in seas like this is very difficult. I was constantly working the throttle and wheel, moving in and out of the sea troughs in between each and every wave. The trick is to climb each wave as it heads into you at an angle (not directly into the wave) and then descend the wave on the other side without falling off and slamming the bow into the next trough. You have to do this on each wave every time, or the ride will be much rougher than it otherwise needs to be.

About five miles offshore, the boat slammed down quite hard coming off of a wave and I began hearing shouting coming from behind me from one of my crew members. I throttled back and stopped the boat to see what was wrong. I grabbed my flashlight from my waistband and turned around and shone the light on the floor of the boat behind my seat. Our screenwriter had apparently forgotten what I said about keeping his knees bent at all times. He was screaming in pain while my crew mates moved in closer to see where he was hurt. I then moved my light to his legs and immediately saw the reason for all the screaming. His shinbone was sticking out of his pants leg. I immediately radioed Papa-100 and told them that our VIP had sustained a compound fracture of his leg and that we needed the paramedics and an ambulance to meet us back at the dock.

Our problem now was how to negotiate these same seas going back (now following seas) without causing more damage. We unhooked the boat's "bumpers" (large pads normally hung over the side of the boat when docking so the boat doesn't impact with a dock) and wedged them on both sides of his leg. We also used our life vests for more padding and tried to make him as comfortable as possible for the trip back. It took almost an hour to make it back, but I'm sure it seemed much longer for him. I never saw him again after that night, but a couple of years later his movie did get made. It wasn't very good, from what I remember.

Bay Side is a beautiful dockside area in downtown Miami with lots of shops and restaurants. We all liked to pull in there and grab lunch, especially when the weather was nice (which was most of the time). I pulled out of there one beautiful Sunday afternoon after eating lunch and saw a friend of mine, Paul Teachy, on his sailboat enjoying the perfect weather. "Teach" worked for Piedmont Airlines at the time and had taken out two flight attendant friends of his for a sail. As we moved away from Bay Side and out into Biscayne Bay, I pulled up alongside of him to chat. He introduced his two friends, who were admiring our go-fast boat, to my crew mate and me. I asked them if they wanted to go for a quick ride. They said they'd love to. As they were stepping over from the sailboat onto ours, I looked over and noticed that Teach had a camera out and was taking a picture.

"Hey," I said. "That picture better not get out. You could get me in a lot of trouble," I told him.

"Don't worry," he said. "I'll make sure you get the only copy."

Sure enough, I saw him about a week later and he gave me the photo.

The picture showed two young ladies in very skimpy bikinis standing on the bow of our boat, with my crewmate and me clearly in the shot. Also quite visible was what was painted on the side of the boat, "US Customs–Police." I then had what I thought was a great idea. I took the picture to the office that night and, after blacking out our faces with a black marker, I made three or four copies and pasted them up around the office where I knew the supervisors would find them. When I came to the office the next day, I found my supervisor sitting at his desk with a magnifying glass trying to discern which of his agents were in the photo.

"If I ever figure out who this is, I'm going to have them fired!" he told me. "Dave, take a look and see if you can tell who this is."

I took the magnifying glass and looked very intently at the picture. "I don't know, Joe," I told him. "Looks like the faces have been blotted out."

Nobody ever found out.

The best prank I pulled was the time that they were making the movie I previously referred to about drug smuggling. They wanted to use some of our go-fast boats for some of the background footage. Everybody knew about the movie and most guys wanted to be in it. That's when I had another great idea.

I took some official government stationery and typed out a bogus memo from the head of the Miami office. The memo stated, "Anyone assigned to the Miami Marine Division that wants to be in the movie must see me personally in my office this Wednesday at two o'clock p.m." I then copied his signature from one of the many memos that he used to send out and forged his signature to the bottom of the memo. I then just waited for the commotion. About ten guys lined up outside the boss's office at the appointed day and time, requesting to see him about being in the movie. When he asked why everybody was there, someone showed him the copy of "his" memo.

"This is bullshit!" he exclaimed. "Who the hell wrote this?"

He called his senior staff in and wanted them to find out who the forger was. The supervisors went through the motions of trying to find out, but even they thought it was hilarious. Nobody was ever the wiser.

It was literally impossible not to love the job I was doing. Every day I came into work I knew I would be spending the next eight hours or so driving around the waters of South Florida in a speedboat and not have to pay for the gas. Since the statute of limitations has run its course (and I'm now retired), I don't mind owning up to the fact that I didn't always follow the rules as they pertained to the "authorized" use of government property.

My roommate at that time was my childhood friend Allen Chapman. Many times when I drove my boat on the midnight shift, Allen and his brother Mark used to meet me at Monty Trainer's in Coconut Grove (a popular dockside bar and restaurant). I would let them come aboard and we would go for a late-night cruise around Biscayne Bay. Mark would sometimes bring along some flight attendant friends of his that he worked with back then. Believe me when I tell you that my high-performance speedboat was the ultimate "chick magnet" (for Allen and Mark, that is).

I had other ideas back then. One of the boats assigned to me as "my boat" during my tenure as boat captain was an unmarked thirty-five-foot cigarette boat that I kept docked at the Miami Marriott Hotel. I could take the boat out anytime I wanted, day or night, but I wasn't supposed to allow any unauthorized people on the boat. I could get in big trouble for that. But I had begun dating a beautiful young lady named Melissa, and I thought how impressed she would be with me if I invited her out for a ride. I took her down to the Marriott one beautiful Sunday afternoon (I knew all of the bosses would be off on a Sunday) and we took the boat out. The seas were calm and the weather could not have been more perfect for a boat ride. We spent a couple of hours on the water, and I even let her drive it. We got it back to the dock without anyone finding out about my unauthorized passenger. A couple of years later I talked her into marrying me, so I guess it was worth the risk!

IV. DRUG AND MONEY-LAUNDERING TASK FORCE

IN 1989 MY BOATING CAREER CAME TO AN END, AND I WAS transferred to a money-laundering task force comprised of special agents from US Customs, the IRS, DEA, and some state and local officers who had been assigned on loan to the task force. The term "money laundering" is derived from the concept of "washing" money that is "dirty." In other words, laundering money occurs by taking money that has been derived from illegal activity (specifically, the selling of illegal drugs) and laundering the money in such a way as to conceal the source and/or ownership of the money from authorities. The drug trade in the '80s and '90s, especially in South Florida, created massive windfalls of cash for people involved in the selling of drugs. Congress passed the Money Laundering Control Act of 1986 to give us investigators a tool to combat the illegal drug trade by going after their profits.

While marijuana smuggling and trafficking were certainly going on back then, as well as the sale and use of other illegal substances like heroin, amphetamines, and the like, the biggest drug problem during this time was cocaine. Almost all of the world's cocaine was produced in South America due to the favorable climate needed to grow the coca plant that is used in the production of cocaine. Once the cocaine was produced, smugglers would transport their "load" to the US and attempt to smuggle it into this country. Much of it reached the US through the Mexican border as well as South Florida. Once it got inside the US, it would be passed along to distributers who would break it down further into smaller loads and then pass it along even further to the street dealers (or pushers) who would make the actual sales to users. There would be several layers between the producers in South America and the pushers in the US. As all of the street sales were made over time, a large amount of cash would begin to pile up. All of this cash would eventually work its way back up the line, with everyone taking his cut, until the South American producers (primarily Colombians) were paid.

The problem that the traffickers had was how to handle the massive amounts of cash so that everyone got paid without law enforcement authorities becoming aware that the money was made from the illegal drug trade. The traffickers primarily accomplished this in one of two ways: getting the money into the US banking system, or smuggling the cash out of the country and into offshore banks where banking laws and regulations were much more lax. Once either of these was accomplished, the money would officially be "washed," or "laundered." It would simply become an accounting line on a bank statement, with no indication that the money was the result of drug trafficking. The money could then be wired from bank to bank around the world and eventually end up in the Colombian bank account (after the conversion from US dollar to pesos) of the cocaine producers.

Traffickers had many hurdles to overcome to accomplish this. First of all, US banking laws required that cash deposits of $10,000 or more be reported to the IRS on a CTR (currency transaction report). Filling out this form would create a paper trail that the traffickers wanted to avoid. A way that some money launderers used to get around this was to utilize a method known as "structuring" (we also called this "smurfing"). To accomplish this, low-level money couriers would be given large amounts of cash and would drive around to banks all over Miami and make deposits of less than $10,000 in multiple accounts, all controlled by one person or group. In the Al Pacino movie *Scarface*, there is a scene where men get out of a van in front of a bank with huge duffel bags full of cash and take them inside for deposit. In real life this was not feasible with all of the banking laws in place and the push by law enforcement to clamp down on money laundering.

Smuggling large amounts of cash out of the country in cargo bins or secreted inside personal luggage was also often attempted. Possession of cash, regardless of the amount, was in and of itself NOT illegal. But the traffickers did not want to file a "declaration" with US Customs, as was required by law for transporting more than $10,000 in cash or negotiable instruments into or out of the country. Again, this created a paper trail that the traffickers wanted to avoid at all cost by not having someone's name attached to the cash on the reporting form filed with the government.

I became the manager of an undercover money-laundering operation known as "Operation FREEZE." This operation was specifically designed to go after the illegal assets (primarily cash) made by traffickers selling illegal drugs in the US. "Oscar" and "Marty" (not their real names) were two brothers of Colombian descent with ties to Colombian traffickers. They were also registered informants of the US Customs Service, and I was their controlling agent. The ultimate success of Operation FREEZE relied heavily on the use of these informants. The traffickers needed someone in the US who could take possession of large amounts of cash and successfully transfer the money via the banking system out of the country and into the trafficker's accounts. What the traffickers didn't know was that the bank accounts used by our informants were actually undercover US Customs bank accounts. In order to accomplish what we were trying to do, it required us to be the money launderers.

The way this operation worked was actually simple in its concept. Oscar would receive a call on his pager from an "unknown" wanting to arrange a money pickup. This money would inevitably be a large amount of cash consolidated in one place, the result of perhaps hundreds of individual street sales of cocaine. As the amount of cash grew, the traffickers needed to get the money out of the country and into the hands of the producers in Colombia. Oscar would return the call and set up a meeting, usually in a large parking lot, where the transfer of money would take place. At the appointed time, an undercover agent working with our task force would show up at the meeting spot and take possession of the cash, usually in boxes or large duffel bags, and then depart. A surveillance team would then follow the money courier away and stay with him the remainder of the day, making note of places he stopped and eventually "putting him to bed" (following him to his place of residence). The money that was picked up would then be deposited in our undercover accounts and transferred out in accordance with the transfer instructions Oscar received from the traffickers.

The money couriers, being used to making these cash hand-offs all over South Florida, were low-level people who knew little or nothing about the traffickers they were working for. This was by design so that if they were ever caught they wouldn't be able to "rat" out the true owners of the money. They usually had no idea who it was that called them in the first place to have them pick up the money and make the delivery to our informant. Our surveillance of the courier would give us the intel of who he was, where he lived, and what car he drove.

Eventually, this same courier would call Oscar again on his pager. When this occurred, I would instruct Oscar to just ignore the page. Using the intel from the previous pickup, we would then go to the guy's house and set up on him and wait for him to move. We knew that the reason he paged Oscar in the first place was because he had another load of money to hand off. By us ignoring his page, we knew that he would eventually call someone else to arrange the delivery of the money. Inevitably, he would make other arrangements and we would just follow him around town until we saw him meet with some other "unknown" and hand off the bags or boxes of cash (exactly as he had done with Oscar). We would then follow the "new" guy away from this meeting and wait for him to get a few miles away before making a traffic stop and seizing the bags of money that he had just picked up. By doing it this way, the bad guys would just assume that we had been following this "new" guy all along and that it was him (and not Oscar) at fault for their money getting seized. In my four years with Operation FREEZE, we worked dozens and dozens of cases just like this that ultimately resulted in the seizure of over $150 million of drug profits.

Woody Kirk was the supervisor of our undercover money-laundering group and the best supervisor I ever worked for. He taught me a lot about how to manage people and resources. He also was a manager that knew how to get the most out of his employees. Our group produced a lot of good cases back then and Woody allowed us quite a bit of freedom without micromanaging our every move. Years later when I became a supervisor, I modeled much of how I supervised on what I learned from watching Woody.

Our operation was funded directly by trafficker funds and not taxpayer money. Taking a small cut of every pickup we did and leaving it in our undercover account accomplished this. We would then transfer the money over to Oscar for him to make his disbursement to the traffickers. Oscar received calls to do pickups in other US cities as well. Besides Miami, we did pickups in Houston, Los Angeles, Chicago, and New York. Our undercover accounts were flush with money, totaling over a million dollars at any one time.

We did have kind of a hiccup once in Houston. After doing a pickup of $300,000, we deposited the money into our Houston bank account as we always did. Our intention was to wire transfer the money out the following day to all the places it needed to go. However, unbeknownst to us, the bank we used was on the verge of collapse, and that afternoon federal bank regulators came in and shut the bank down. At that time all accounts were federally insured up to $100,000, but everything over that amount was at risk of being lost in a bank shut down. Our operation took a $200,000 hit! Needless to say, the bosses were not too pleased. The special-agent-in-charge for Miami (my ultimate boss) had me in his office the next morning. He instructed me to make sure that our undercover accounts never had balances of over $100,000 from now on, even if that meant opening up additional accounts to spread the money around.

Oscar called me one afternoon and told me that he had just gotten a call asking him if he could do a pickup in Sydney, Australia.

"Are you serious?" I said.

Of course, all I was thinking about was how cool it would be to go to Australia. I told him I'd get back to him as soon as possible and immediately ran it up the chain to see what the reaction would be. Everybody was on board, and I began coordinating with Customs Headquarters in Washington to make it happen. Because it was international, I knew there would be a lot of red tape and hoops to jump through if we were going to pull this off. Once I got headquarters to buy in, I told Oscar to call them back and tell them he could do it. My headquarters contact made all the necessary arrangements with the US Embassy in Canberra, Australia, and the pickup was set up.

The first thing I needed to do when I arrived in Australia was go to a meeting with the director of the AFP (Australian Federal Police). They had no experience with money-laundering cases and very little experience working large-scale drug cases.

"We don't really have a drug problem here like you do in the US," he told me at our first meeting.

He asked me to explain what exactly our operation wanted to do. I told him that we had received a call from Colombian traffickers that wanted us to pick up Six hundred thousand dollars in drug proceeds for us to launder.

"Six hundred thousand dollars of drug profits, here in Sydney?" he asked incredulously. "Not possible," he declared.

I told him the plan was to pick up three hundred thousand dollars one day and then the other three hundred thousand dollars the following day.

"Once that's done," I told him, "I'm going to need to deposit the money in the bank and then wire transfer it to our undercover account back in the States." I then explained that his investigators could continue following the guy we met with and develop their own case on him after we were gone.

I'm sure he thought I was crazy, that there could not possibly be $600,000 worth of drug sales in all of Australia, much less there in Sydney, so he agreed to let us make the pickup. I told Oscar to arrange for the pickup to be in front of the Sydney Opera House (just because I thought that would be so cool) the following day. After we did the pickup, I took the gym bag with $300,000 in Australian dollars and opened it up in the director's office. His eyes opened like saucers and he put both hands to the sides of his head.

"My God!" he exclaimed. "There can't possibly be more than that."

"Actually, we're picking up another $300,000 tomorrow," I replied.

And we did.

About two weeks later I received a call from my AFP counterpart, Alan, who worked with us the whole time we were in Sydney. As it turned out, the AFP continued surveilling the guy that had delivered the money to Oscar and identified several apartments he visited. They then raided those apartments and subsequently made the largest seizure of cocaine in the history of Australian law enforcement. Alan said that the director would like to know if we wanted to come back and do it all over again.

"He's a believer now," said Alan.

Two months later, Oscar got another call for a pickup in Sydney and we went back. The results of that second trip were equal to the first, but with one small exception.

One thing I quickly learned on my trips to Sydney was that Australian men did not much like American men. Alan told me it had something to do with that fact that Australian women loved American men because of our accent.

"You're kidding me," I said. "You're the ones with the accent."

One night we were all standing around the bar at a local pub in downtown Sydney, swapping stories and enjoying pints of Foster, when this local guy at the bar turned around and made some snarky comment about Americans. We all ignored him and just kept on with our evening. As we began to leave some minutes later, I noticed this same guy follow us out of the bar and onto the sidewalk outside. As we walked up the street, he stayed right behind us and began taunting us, directing his comments at me. I didn't know it at the time, but two uniformed police officers were directly across the street witnessing what was going on. They suspected there might be trouble, so they immediately made their way to our side of the street.

All of a sudden the guy shoved me from behind, obviously looking to start a fight. When I spun around the guy swung a fist at me that I was able to duck under. As I rose up, ready to defend myself, my "lights" were literally knocked out. As Alan explained to me later (after I came to), one of the cops had seen the guy shove me from behind and took out his baton and moved in. After the guy swung at me, the cop raised his baton intending to hit the guy, but instead missed and caught me square on top of my head. He was very apologetic afterwards, especially after Alan identified himself to the cops and told them who I was. We had a pretty good laugh over that.

Here's a blatant example of just how screwed up and political it can get working for the government. The two pickups we made in Sydney were hugely successful and resulted in record drug seizures for the AFP. They definitely wanted us to come back for at least a third time, if not more after that. But here was the problem: US Customs did not have a representative in the US Embassy in Canberra. Our attaché that covered Australia was in Singapore, not Australia. The DEA, however, had a representative in Canberra. They also had the ear of the DCM (Deputy Chief of Mission). The DCM is the one that calls all the shots and must give his approval for us to come there and conduct official business, which he had done the previous two trips. But now the DEA wanted more of a hand in the operation since it was related to drugs, and especially because it had proven to be highly successful.

Word got back to me from my headquarters contact that DEA now wanted to be in charge of the operation and that approval for a third trip would not be granted unless I turned my informant over to them and allowed them to run the operation in Australia. I told headquarters to tell DEA thanks, but no thanks. No way was that going to happen. Informants are without a doubt one of the most valuable assets any investigator has and no way was I going to cede that asset to another agency. And so that ended our case in Australia. Who knows how much more success could have occurred had we continued, but politics got in the way. The DEA would rather have had the case shut down than have it continue without them getting to claim the credit. It was really pathetic. Believe me, stuff like that happens all the time!

During the 1990s our operation became truly international in its scope. Besides Australia, we expanded our pickup operation to Canada, Spain, and Austria. The money that dopers were making from the cocaine trade during this time was exploding exponentially all over the world. Subsequently, their need to find innovative ways to launder their proceeds was also growing. Selling dollars on the black market was another way to launder drug profits that was gaining prominence. It was also a way the Colombians could maximize their profits. Buying and selling dollars on the black market was a way that the Colombian cartels could avoid paying the high exchange rate that the Colombian government charged when exchanging US dollars into Colombian pesos. Since US dollars were worthless to the Colombians in Colombia, they had to convert the dollars to pesos. One US dollar was equal to about five thousand pesos back then.

The government would take by way of a "tax" (their exchange fee), around 7 or 8 percent of the total amount of the currency conversion. In other words, if a Colombian cocaine producer had a million dollars' worth of profit on his drug sales in the US, it would cost him about seventy or eighty thousand dollars in exchange fees to get his money converted to pesos and into his Colombian bank account using the normal banking system. Selling his dollars on the black market could save him millions in profits.

Here's an example of how this black market system would work:

A Colombian trafficker has five million in US dollars, all made from cocaine sales, hidden at a "stash house" in Miami. He needs to get that money to him in Colombia, not in US dollars but in pesos. A Colombian businessman needs to purchase five million dollars' worth of tractors from a John Deere plant in Ocala, Florida, and have the tractors shipped to him in Colombia. The tractors would have to be purchased in the US using US dollars. The two men would reach an agreement whereby the trafficker would sell five million in US dollars to the businessman for an exchange rate of, say, 4 percent. Both men would save on the transaction, because they would both avoid the high exchange rate that the Colombian government would charge.

The businessman in Colombia would then give the trafficker pesos equal to five million US dollars (minus the 4 percent exchange fee) and deposit that into the trafficker's Colombian bank account. The businessman would then give the trafficker bank account information and wiring instructions to his US bank account in Florida where the five million dollars located at the stash house was to be sent. Once all transactions are completed, the businessman will have his money in his US bank account to purchase his tractors and the trafficker will have his drug profits in his Colombian bank account in pesos. Our operation facilitated these transactions by being the conduit by which the money at the stash house was picked up, deposited into the US banking system, and subsequently wire transferred to the Colombian businessman's US bank account. As was the case with all of the pickups we did, extensive surveillance was done following each pickup to gather intel on the groups involved in stockpiling the huge amounts of money made in the cocaine trade.

Our money-laundering investigative group was incredibly busy in the '90s. As already mentioned, we were doing money pickups all over the US, as well as several cities overseas. The cases generated from the intel gained from all of this activity were overwhelming. Because money-laundering operations by US Customs Agents were fairly new, it seemed we were making up the rules as we went along. On many occasions I participated in the surveillance of a money courier we had identified from a previous pickup and ended up making a car stop and subsequent seizure of bags of cash. I would then throw the money in the backseat of my car and drive back to the office, where we all would do a count of the money and process all of the required reports documenting the seizure. I was never tempted to take a bundle or two off the top while driving back to the office, but it didn't escape me how easy it would have been to simply grab two or three stacks of cash and toss them under the seat for later retrieval. Nobody would've known because no one knew how much money we seized because it hadn't been counted yet.

Even with adequate safeguards in place, there was always going to be the possibility of being accused of corruption. Rolando Fernandez was a doper and money launderer we had been working on for some time. Our group got a search warrant for his house that we subsequently executed. I grabbed my flashlight, climbed up on his kitchen counter, and pushed up some ceiling tiles to search the area above his drop ceiling. I spotted a large bag hidden up there and retrieved it. It contained $300,000 in cash that we subsequently seized. About a month later I was called into the office and shown a letter mailed to US Customs from Fernandez's lawyer. The letter was contending that the seizure was unjust and that the source of the money we seized from Fernandez was legitimate. The letter also stated that the amount of cash that Mr. Fernandez had in the bag we seized was $350,000, not $300,000 as we had claimed. His lawyer was making an obvious inference that someone had stolen $50,000 from his client. Thankfully his specious charge went nowhere because of all the witnesses.

My good friend and fellow agent Steve Wunderlich once loaded the trunk of his car with five or six gym bags full of cash from a seizure made from doing a car stop in South Miami. Steve and the other agents drove to the office and after arriving, quickly grabbed the bags from the trunk and went inside. The bags contained about $600,000 in drug proceeds, and all of the necessary seizure forms were filled out and the money was properly turned in to the seizure clerk. Three or four days later, Steve opened the trunk of his car to put something away when he noticed an unfamiliar gym bag in the back of the trunk. He was gripped by fear when he realized where the bag came from.

He pulled it out and unzipped the bag and found multiple stacks of cash inside totaling about $100,000. He and the other agents had simply missed it when they unloaded the trunk a few days earlier and taken the gym bags inside the office for processing. Steve did the right thing and immediately notified our supervisor and took the cash to the office where it was properly processed and added to the seizure totals from the previous day. But it highlighted the need for better safeguards to avoid corruption on the part of we agents who were handling hundreds of thousands of dollars in uncounted drug money. What if Steve wasn't completely honest? What if he had just kept his mouth shut and not said anything to anyone? Nobody would've ever known about the bag. As far as any of us knew, the bags originally taken into the office from Steve's trunk were all the bags that were seized and the cash total from that original count was the extent of the seizure made that day.

Years later when I worked in the financial division at our headquarters in Washington, I participated in a group tasked with writing policy that would govern all undercover money-laundering operations. One of the first things I recommended was a rule mandating that seized currency would always be transported by at least two agents to help avoid some of the potential problems I had experienced.

I was once acting supervisor of our group when I got a call from the airport that Customs inspectors had found $250,000 in cash secreted inside two microwave ovens that had been checked luggage for an outbound flight to Colombia. Steve Wunderlich was in the office, so I asked him if he would go to the airport and work the case. When Steve arrived at the airport, he spoke to the inspectors and then retrieved all of the necessary passenger manifest information to try and determine to whom the microwave ovens belonged. The luggage tags that coincided with the ovens indicated that they belonged to an elderly man from Johnson City, Tennessee. His ticket information also indicated that he was due to return to Miami two weeks later.

What Steve did not know at the time was that the American Airlines ticket agent that had assigned the luggage tags to Mr.

Johnson City was corrupt. He had been paid by the money launderers to check the ovens in and assign them to someone OTHER than the individual who had actually brought them to the airport. The ticket agent simply grabbed a random name off the passenger manifest for that flight and entered his name into the system as being the owner of the suspect ovens. The bad guys knew that Mr. Johnson City would not be looking to pick up the two microwave ovens once they landed in Colombia. Instead, the guy that actually did check them in could pick them up upon arrival from the baggage claim area and didn't have to risk being caught in Miami if, indeed, the Customs inspectors in Miami found the cash.

Two weeks later when Mr. Johnson City was due to return to Miami, Steve went to the airport to meet him. The US Attorney had authorized Steve to arrest the guy as soon as he set foot on US soil. It just so happened that his return trip to Miami coincided with a Dolphins-Jets game that Steve had tickets for later that afternoon. He calculated that if the flight arrived on time, he had just barely enough time to arrest the guy when he got off the plane, transport him to the Miami Federal Detention Facility, and still make the game by kickoff. But he was going to have to hurry.

The elderly Mr. Johnson City was obviously surprised when Steve approached him in the arrivals area and identified himself as a US Customs agent with a warrant for his arrest. He had gone down to Colombia for a two-week hunting trip and had no idea why he was now being detained (and for good reason, since he knew nothing about the cash in the microwaves and was completely innocent). As Steve was rushing to get him locked up so he could make the game by kickoff, Mr. Johnson City started having chest pains in the car on the way to jail.

Now Steve's thinking, *Oh, great, now I'm going to have to take him to the hospital first. I'll never make the game.*

Steve asked the gentleman, "Do you have any pills or anything you can take?"

"I've got some nitro pills in my bag," he replied.

Steve pulled over on the side of the road and went into the guy's bag and found the pills. Since the guy was handcuffed, Steve had to place two of the little pills under the guy's tongue while they sat on the side of the road.

"Feel any better?" Steve asked him.

"I think so," he replied.

So off they went to jail. Steve processed the guy in and then made it to the game just before kickoff.

Within a couple of days, it was determined that this guy had nothing to do with the cash in the microwaves. He had, in fact, been the innocent victim of the corrupt ticket agent who had assigned his name to the luggage tags for the ovens containing all of the cash. Steve called the American Airlines office to arrange an interview with the suspect ticket agent. He was told that the guy had not shown up for work the past few days and no one had any idea where he was. In fact, the guy had gotten wind that federal agents wanted to talk to him and he immediately left the country, never to be heard from or seen again. As far as Mr. Johnson City goes, he ended up suing the US government and American Airlines and collected . . . *seven million dollars* for his trouble! Not too bad for having to spend a night or two in jail for something he didn't do.

There was another money case Steve and I worked together that proved somewhat interesting. One of Steve's informants had told him that he had received a page from a target wanting to make a delivery of cash. We already knew where this target lived because he had delivered money to this informant previously. We told the informant not to return the call, hoping to get on the target's tail and make a seizure. We sat in front of his house and saw him and a young lady carry several gym bags from the house and place them in the trunk of his car. After loading all of the bags, he kissed the woman and then got in his car and drove away. Steve and I then followed him away from the house. After following him for several miles, we decided to conduct a car stop. We got consent to search his trunk and retrieved the gym bags, which contained about $400,000 in cash.

Steve and I took the seizure back to the office for processing, took a Polaroid picture of the guy, and then counted and bagged the money. We then returned to the house, thinking there might be more money still inside that we could add to the seizure. We knocked on the door and the female we had seen earlier opened the door. After identifying ourselves as federal agents, we asked her if she would allow us to come inside and search her house. She told us that she would not allow us in and that she wanted to call her lawyer, which she did.

While waiting for the lawyer to show up, I asked one of the task force agents assisting us to sit in front of the house. Steve and I wanted to get a search warrant for the house and while we were gone, wanted to make sure nobody removed anything else from the house. When we returned a couple of hours later with the warrant, we knocked on the door. This time the lady's lawyer answered the door and let us in after we showed him the warrant. Before we began our search, Steve told the female that we had seen some guy leave the house earlier that morning and asked her whom it was.

"I don't know what you're talking about," she said. "There wasn't anybody else here this morning."

Steve then pulled out the Polaroid. "This is the guy," he said, showing the picture to the woman.

"I've never seen him before," she said. "I don't know who that is."

Steve and I then conducted our search with the lawyer beside us the whole time. Steve opened up a dresser drawer in the bedroom and found an envelope that contained several pictures. Steve called me in to look at them with him, along with the attorney. The photos were highly pornographic in nature and were pictures of the female in the other room with the guy she had just told us she didn't know!

Steve looked back at the lawyer and asked, "I thought she said she didn't know this guy. Does she always act like this with people she doesn't know?"

The lawyer had no reply. We continued our search and found several cardboard boxes slid underneath the bed that contained almost $1 million in drug money. We loaded the boxes in our cars and then left.

I was truly amazed at some of the things the couriers we seized money from would tell us. On one particular case, I remember watching a guy we were surveilling load brown paper grocery bags into the backseat of his car. We knew he was a money courier and were confident that the bags probably contained cash. After following him around town for a while, we decided to do a car stop. When I approached his driver-side door, I looked in the back window and could see five grocery bags on the backseat, each one filled to the top with bundles of cash. After identifying myself to the driver as a federal agent, I asked him where he was going.

"I'm on my way to the store," he said.

"What are you buying today?" I asked.

"Just some groceries," he replied.

"Looks like you've already been to the grocery store," I commented as I pointed to the bags in the backseat.

The guy then turned around and looked in the backseat. Trying to act completely surprised, he then said, "I've never seen those bags before. I don't know whose they are."

"But they're in your car," I said.

"Oh," he replied. "This isn't my car."

"Well if it's not your car, then I guess those aren't your bags?" I said.

"That's right," he said. "Those aren't my bags. This car belongs to a friend of mine," he said.

"What's your friend's name?" I asked him.

"I don't know her name," he then told me. "I just met her this morning!"

One time we got word through one of our informants that a courier was transporting $800,000 in cash from New York to Miami via Amtrak. He was taking the train all the way down because the inspection of luggage (where all the cash was stored) was less stringent than it would be if he were flying. The courier's name was Francisco Valdez and he was Colombian. I had one of our group's analysts check the passenger manifests of all of the New York to Miami trips over the upcoming few weeks, looking for Valdez's name. We found it. Another agent and I drove up to West Palm Beach and bought tickets for the train that we knew Valdez would be on so we could ride with him down to Miami. We knew that he was Colombian, midtwenties, and that he would be wearing a gray sports jacket. That was all the description our informant could give us.

After boarding the train in West Palm Beach, we walked up and down the aisles of each train car, looking for someone who fit that description. We spotted a guy sitting by himself in one of the forward cars that we were 90 percent sure was him. We found some seats in that car and kept an eye on him for the rest of the trip to Miami. This was in the early days of cell phones. They were large gray phones known as "bricks." I had one and was able to keep in contact with agents waiting at the station in Miami.

After arriving in Miami, Valdez retrieved a large suitcase from his overhead bin area and stepped off the train with me and another agent behind him. As we walked through the terminal, I approached him from behind and stopped him. I told him we were US Customs agents looking for people transporting drugs into South Florida and would like to talk to him. Of course, we already knew he wasn't transporting drugs. He knew it too, so he was all too willing to give me consent to search his luggage for drugs, which we both knew he wasn't carrying.

Getting consent to search in this case (and almost all of the enforcement stops we made) was imperative. Getting a warrant would mean swearing to an affidavit that contained identifying information about our informant. This would "burn" him and put his life in danger, so obtaining consent from the target was the only way to legally do our search. Fortunately for us, virtually every money courier I ever encountered agreed to give consent for a search. This was primarily due to the fact that the money didn't belong to them, and probably because they weren't aware of the fact that they could refuse. Valdez was no exception. He told me he didn't have any drugs and that I could look inside his suitcase just to be sure. He opened his suitcase for me, only to reveal several bundles of neatly stacked hundred-dollar bills. Valdez told me that he had no idea whose money it was. He said that he had been given the suitcase in New York, didn't know it contained money, and was asked to deliver it to someone in Miami.

We took Valdez and the suitcase to our office and counted and seized the currency. The tally was exactly $800,000 as our informant had said. Even though we knew it was drug money, we had to release Valdez, because to arrest him would have meant exposing our informant. We were happy just to make the seizure and rob the dopers of some of their profit. Before releasing him, I took a photo of Valdez holding up a bumper sticker that my friend and colleague Bob Starkman had made up that said, "So Many Colombians, So Little Time . . . Operation Greenback."

Bob was quite a character. We called him "Murray the Vendor." He was a Jewish guy from New York that was always peddling little trinkets around the office to make a few extra bucks. The bumper stickers he had made up were most certainly not politically correct, but we thought they were hilarious.

Besides the politically incorrect bumper sticker, Bob was also famous for his creation of the "Writ of Hocus Pocus." As was the case with virtually every currency seizure we made, the guy we nabbed with the cash would never claim ownership and would never acknowledge knowing the name of the true owner. Bob would simply present him with an official-looking form and tell the guy, "This is a writ of hocus pocus. Sign this and we make the money disappear."

What he was actually signing was an abandonment form, waiving all future claims to ownership of the money. This made the forfeiture of the money to the US government go much quicker, since there would be nobody with standing to come in later and claim that the money belonged to them.

There's no doubt that some of the people we seized money from did not live a long and prosperous life after losing the money that they had been entrusted with. I remember one guy sitting down at his kitchen table and putting his head in his hands, obviously distraught about us removing several hundred thousand dollars in cash that he was supposed to take care of.

He looked up at me and said, "Can I get some kind of receipt from you? I don't know how I'm going to explain losing all of this money," he said.

I looked around his kitchen and found a pad of notebook paper on the table. I took out a pen and wrote across the top of the paper, "US Customs seized several boxes of currency on this date from Mr. Gonzalez." I then scribbled down a made-up signature and the date, and then handed the piece of paper to him.

He just looked at me as if to say, "Are you kidding? This is it?" I'm not sure if that receipt helped him stay out of trouble or not . . . probably not!

Many of our surveillances took us to Miami International Airport, where our money targets would attempt to smuggle cash out of the country. As already stated, simply possessing cash was in and of itself not a crime, no matter the amount. But since federal law required that a report be filed with US Customs if someone was transporting more than $10,000 in or out of the US, many of our targets attempted to smuggle cash out without filing the necessary declaration. Once an individual checked in at the airport ticket counter, obtained their boarding pass for an international flight, and checked their luggage, they were deemed to have articulated their intentions to leave the country. These acts would necessitate their responsibility to file a currency declaration if, in fact, they were transporting more than the $10,000 limit.

When we followed a target to the airport, at least one agent would stand in line behind the suspect and radio to me and other agents a description of the luggage that had been checked at the ticket counter. We would be waiting in the baggage area behind and/or underneath the ticket counter area where all baggage would pass through after being checked. This was the area where airline baggage handlers would pull bags off of the conveyer belts and load them onto baggage carts to take them to the outbound planes.

Once we got a description of the suspect bag, we would intercept the bag before it got loaded onto the baggage cart and open it up right there on the ground of the baggage area beneath the conveyer belts. We seized millions of dollars in cash doing this. Sometimes the cash would just be packed away inside of zipped compartments within the suitcase. More often than not they would make more of an effort to conceal the cash. We found it sewn into the linings of jackets; stuffed inside children's toys; or secreted behind false panels of the suitcase itself. I always wondered how fun it would have been to have seen the looks on the faces of these people when they got to their destination, only to discover that their luggage didn't make it.

You don't always have to be a great investigator to make a really good case. There is no better example of this than what happened to me and another agent one afternoon. Several other agents had gathered in the office and were getting ready to go out on surveillance. The lead agent for this case had more than enough help, but the other agent and I weren't really doing anything so we just volunteered to go along. We told the lead agent that we would just find some nice, quiet place a few miles from the target's house and just hang around in case we were needed. I didn't really think we would be needed, but I just thought it would be nice of us to offer.

We drove to a backstreet a couple of miles away from where the surveillance team was setting up and found a nice, shady spot to sit. We parked our cars about fifty feet apart and just sat there, monitoring the radio traffic from the guys that were set up on the target's house. As I sat in my car, I noticed a guy standing at a bank of pay phones situated in the rear of a gas station parking lot about thirty yards from where I sat. He was dropping quarters in each of the pay phones, making quick calls, and then hanging up. I immediately recognized that what he was doing was dialing people's pagers, hanging up, and then waiting for them to return his call.

This was in the days before cell phones became so widespread. Dopers would routinely use pay phones to make contact with other dopers to arrange for pickups of either money or dope. They used pay phones instead of personal landlines so their calls couldn't be tapped or traced by law enforcement. I picked up my radio mike and called the other agent.

"Are you watching that guy on the pay phones?" I asked him.

"I was just about to call you and ask you the same thing," he replied.

We both decided to just keep watching him and see what he did. I figured if he was setting up a meet, he might lead the other guy right to where we were.

After about fifteen minutes, the guy left the pay phones and got in his car that was parked nearby. We then decided to go talk to him. When I got to his driver-side window, I tapped on the glass, showed him my badge, and motioned for him to roll down his window. I told him that we were federal agents and that there had been complaints of drug dealing in the area (a complete lie). I asked him what he was doing there and if he was waiting on someone. He told me that he wasn't waiting on anybody and that he was just resting. I then asked him if he would mind popping his trunk and letting us take a look inside.

"Oh, no problem, sir," he said. "It's not my car anyway."

He got out of the car and walked to the trunk and opened it for us to look inside. We immediately saw three large, green duffel bags.

"What's in the bags?" I asked him.

"I don't know," he said. "Like I told you, this isn't my car."

"Well whose car is it?" I asked.

"I don't know the guy's name," he said. "It's just someone I met the other day. He let me borrow his car."

We then reached in and unzipped the first bag, revealing several bricks of cocaine. The other two bags were also filled with cocaine. We arrested the guy and took him into custody. We then took the duffel bags to the office and processed the seizure. The total seizure we made that day was fifty-five kilograms of cocaine. It was without a doubt the easiest case I ever made!

In June of 1989 I came into the office to clean up some paperwork before taking off for two weeks of leave. That lady I had given that boat ride to a couple years earlier had agreed to marry me, and our wedding was set to take place in about a week. This was my last day in the office before taking off, and I just wanted to get some paperwork done and then get the heck out of there. One of the agents in our group, Ron Ingleby, had been working a case on a guy named Juan Ochoa and asked me if I wanted to go with him and some other agents to his house and help arrest him. He was involved in both money laundering and drug trafficking and was supposedly a cousin of Jorge Ochoa, who, along with Pablo Escobar, founded the Medellin Cartel. Escobar was known as the "King of Cocaine" and the Medellin Cartel was responsible for most of the world's cocaine production at that time. Getting a family member of Jorge Ochoa would certainly be notable.

I was glad to go along and help, but I certainly did not want to turn this into an all-night thing. I really just wanted to get through the day and then get out of there, but I also didn't want to leave Ron and the other guys hanging. We all got in our cars and headed to Ft. Lauderdale, where Ochoa lived. What we knew about Ochoa was that he spent most of his days at the gym and most of his nights at a local strip club. It was common for him to drop five or six thousand dollars a night on strippers. We set up on his house and waited for him to come home. After sitting for about four hours with no trace of Ochoa, Ron got on the radio and said he was calling it a day.

Good, I thought. *Now I can get out of here and go home.*

As we began leaving Ochoa's neighborhood, one of the other agents got on the radio and said he just saw Ochoa's car pass him going the other way and that it looked like he was pulling into his neighborhood. We all turned around and headed back to our spots. Ochoa got out of his car with what appeared to be one of his girlfriend-strippers and went inside his house. About thirty minutes later they both came back outside and got in his car to leave. There were four of us in separate cars, and we all got in behind Ochoa and followed him out of his neighborhood. Ron got on the radio and began coordinating how we would take him down.

Ochoa pulled out onto Oakland Park Boulevard, which is a major thoroughfare in Ft. Lauderdale. It was about five thirty in the afternoon, so the traffic was very congested. As we pulled up to a red light, we had two cars directly in front of Ochoa, one directly beside him, and I was in my car directly behind. We had him completely boxed in. As our cars came to a stop, Ron gave the signal to take him down.

We all jumped out of our cars at the same time, guns drawn. One agent pointed a shotgun at Ochoa's driver-side window and yelled for him to raise his hands. The other two agents also pointed their pistols at him through the windshield. I ran around to the passenger door and opened it with my gun pointing at both Ochoa and his girlfriend, who at this point was screaming uncontrollably. I reached in the passenger-side door and grabbed her by the hair and pulled her out onto the sidewalk, all the while keeping my gun pointed at Ochoa. I yelled for her to lie down, which she did, and then dropped one knee onto the center of her back while still aimed in at Ochoa. We pulled Ochoa out of the car and laid him down on the sidewalk beside his girlfriend and then cuffed and arrested him.

A few weeks later, after I had come back from my honeymoon, I saw Ron in the office. He asked me if I heard about what happened to Ochoa. I told him I had not. He told me that the US Marshals were walking him through the Federal Building a few days after we had arrested him and that he broke away from them and tried to kill himself by diving out of a second-story window. His hands were cuffed behind him at the time and he crashed through the window headfirst, landing on the ground below. His attempt at suicide, however, failed. He was relatively unscathed due to the fact that he was such a gym rat and was so muscle-bound from taking steroids that he basically just bounced off the ground without causing much damage. He told one of the US Marshals afterward that he wanted to kill himself because he had so shamed his family name by getting himself arrested.

Some of the "characters" in our group, unfortunately, were not so fun to work with or even be around. Marcy Hines was one of the research analysts assigned to our office as support personnel. All of us agents figured out early on to steer clear of her whenever possible. She was, for lack of a better term, a black militant from somewhere up north. We all got the impression that she didn't much like white people. Even though I was born and raised in Miami, I had been a cop in Alabama before coming on board with Customs, and I think she thought of me as a "Southern white boy." Although I had very little interaction with her when she first began, I got the distinct feeling early on that she did not like me. She loved Bob Starkman for some reason. Everybody loved Bob, but nobody could figure out why Marcy liked him so much. Especially since he used to refer to her as Tawana Brawley to her face. The other nickname that Bob had for her was "Kamala—The Ugandan Giant," which was the real-life name of a professional wrestler. We all thought it fit her to a T.

Everything came to a head one day when my two best friends, Steve Wunderlich and Mike Rich, and I were standing around our cubicles talking about the riots that had just taken place in Los Angeles following the Rodney King incident. Steve and I had just been in LA about a week earlier working with that office on a pickup case that had taken place right where the riots had broken out. We were simply lamenting the fact that had the riots happened a week earlier, we would have responded differently than those who had been victimized by the rioting thugs because we, of course, would have been armed. For some reason this conversation didn't sit well with Marcy.

She got up from her desk and stormed out of the office, leaving the three of us wondering what her problem was. As it turned out, she walked next door to the special-agent-in-charge's office where the bosses were and said she wanted to file a complaint on me. When she was asked what I had done, she told my supervisor that she overheard me say to Steve and Mike that I would have "shot all those niggers" who were rioting in Los Angeles. An obvious lie and one not too difficult to refute, especially since there were at least two witnesses there that knew I had said nothing of the sort. Needless to say, following this incident I tried to avoid Marcy as much as possible.

About a week later I came into the office after being out on surveillance and needed to write a report. I noticed Marcy sitting at my desk using my computer. Desk computers were fairly new back then and not everyone had one. It was common for all of us to share.

As I walked by my desk I said, "Marcy, please get up from my desk, I need my computer," and then departed the immediate area so there would not be any kind of confrontation with her.

She angrily got up and left the office, and then proceeded to go next door to see my supervisor yet again. On this occasion she told my boss that I had just come into the office and told her, "Marcy, get your big, fat, black ass out of my chair," and that it was becoming impossible for her to "work with that racist, David Coppage."

This time there were about five witnesses there who saw and heard everything that happened and, of course, they gave statements that everything Marcy had said was total crap. She was transferred out of group shortly after that. One would think that management would have looked unfavorably on someone making such horrible accusations about another employee, but they took no action against her whatsoever. I'm pretty sure they themselves were afraid of being called racists if they attempted to discipline her for misconduct. If I learned anything over my long career with the federal government, it's that cowardice is in no small supply within the management ranks.

As I mentioned before, our operation was funded by trafficker funds. By this, I mean that each time we did a money pickup, we held back a small percentage of the pickup amount and kept it in our undercover bank account. We used this money to fund all of our travel related to the operation. The Miami bosses liked this because they never had to use their allotted budget to pay for our activities. Because our money-laundering group was making so many seizures of both money and cocaine, we were given a lot of flexibility in deciding what we wanted to do in furtherance of the operation. This occasionally led to the proverbial "boondoggle" trip, as we called it.

One such boondoggle I went on was a trip to Bermuda with another agent, Steve Hayward. Steve was without a doubt the best criminal investigator I ever worked with. He had forgotten more about money-laundering investigations than I would probably ever know, so I worked with him whenever I could. Steve once put together a money-laundering case we all helped him on that resulted in a singular seizure of $22.5 million in cash. The Customs commissioner and other high-ranking officials in Washington, DC, came down to hold a press conference at the Biltmore Hotel in Coral Gables following this record seizure. They wanted to bring attention to our efforts at combating the massive drug trade problem permeating South Florida. This record seizure highlighted some of the success we were enjoying.

Regarding our trip to Bermuda, our stated intention in the travel request was, "to liaison with Bermudan Customs on mutual money-laundering interests." The reality was neither of us had ever been to Bermuda and it sounded like a really cool trip to go on. As I did with almost all of my trips, I took my golf clubs with me. Our hosts in Bermuda set us up at one of the resort golf courses there. We spent a lot of time at the pool of our resort hotel, drinking umbrella drinks. Before leaving, Steve and I decided to treat our hosts and their wives to dinner on the last night we were there. We met at the Fourways Inn restaurant, a very upscale restaurant in Bermuda. I remember being somewhat shocked when I looked at the menu and saw appetizers starting at $30. The final bill for six of us was about $1,800, all paid for from our undercover operation account. We actually did have legitimate discussions about legitimate issues, but don't kid yourself, this trip was a boondoggle.

Another boondoggle trip happened around the time of the 1993 Super Bowl. My best friend and college roommate, Robin Boutwell, called one afternoon and asked me if I would be interested in meeting him in Los Angeles to go to the Super Bowl that was being played in the Rose Bowl between the Dallas Cowboys and the Buffalo Bills (this followed the 1992 NFL season). He had gotten tickets through his job at PepsiCo. I told him most definitely.

I then called Oscar, my informant, and told him he needed to make some calls and arrange to do a pickup in Los Angeles for the week following that Super Bowl Sunday, which he did. The pickup was scheduled for the Monday following the game, so I that we could go to the game. So as it turned out, I got my plane ticket and hotel paid for by the operation, since the trip was legitimately work related, and got to go to the Super Bowl. Robin even comped me my ticket to the game since he stayed in my room with me and didn't have to pay for a hotel room himself. An interesting sidenote of this trip was the fact that our seats at the game were directly behind O. J. Simpson's parents and his wife, Nicole Brown Simpson. Our knees were literally touching them for most of the game. A year and a half later, of course, Simpson murdered Nicole and her friend, which then led to "the trial of the century," as it became known.

There is no doubt that without our confidential informants (CIs), our undercover money-laundering operation could not possibly have attained the results that it did. The contributions of informants in all areas of law enforcement cannot be overstated. A great criminal investigator without a CI will still make a few decent cases. A mediocre criminal investigator with a good CI will make much more. And a great investigator who knows how to recruit and control CIs will make lots of phenomenal cases. They are indispensable. Yes, it is dangerous for them, but it can also be highly financially rewarding.

All of the Customs CIs were required to sign informant agreements between themselves and the government. In the case of the Operation FREEZE CIs, we agreed to pay them compensation commensurate with 10 percent of the seizures that were made and ultimately forfeited to the government. Additionally, the seizure had to be directly attributable to their information. During the four years that I ran Operation FREEZE, we seized approximately $150 million in drug proceeds. Oscar and Marty were not the only CIs that the operation utilized, but they were the primary ones. I personally ended up making CI payments to them that totaled over $11 million. A couple of years after I had left Miami for Washington, DC, Oscar called me to ask if there was any way I could get him working again. The operation had closed down, and he was essentially out of work. He told me that between a few bad business investments and his wife divorcing him, he was almost dead broke. I couldn't help him. He fell off of my radar screen after that, and I moved on with my career and never knew what happened to Oscar or his brother.

Corruption, unfortunately, occurs everywhere in life, and law enforcement is no exception. We handled hundreds and hundreds of thousands of uncounted drug money all the time. I already talked about how easy it could have been for an agent to steal a stack or two of cash if he was so inclined. The temptation was definitely there for some. I never saw it except for one huge and glaring exception.

There were three federal agents that were assigned to our undercover money-laundering group that I had worked with a lot over the years. All three had participated in numerous cases with the rest of us, had gone on surveillance with us, processed seizures with us, and helped serve arrest warrants. Our group was fairly close because we spent so much time with one another, and in some ways it seemed as if we were family. It was for all of these reasons that what happened with these three agents was so heartbreaking.

The three of them worked closely together on several cases. One of these agents had an informant that set up money pickups for our operation. Unbeknownst to any of them, this informant had gone to Customs Internal Affairs (IA) and told them that he knew of some federal agents that were dirty. This informant had run into some trouble and had offered up these agents as a way of getting himself out of trouble.

What became apparent after all was said and done was that this informant had gone to his controlling agent with information about a criminal associate of his that had about $100,000 stashed in his hotel room. He told this agent that he would let him know when this "target" was not in his hotel room and that if the agent wanted, he and his friends (the other two agents) could raid the room and take the money for themselves. What the agents didn't know was that this was actually a "sting" set up by Internal Affairs and that the money inside was government sting money.

This informant had told IA that he had given money and expensive watches to the three agents in the past, which ultimately led to the IA investigation. The three agents raided the room and, just as the informant had predicted, they stole the money. At the time this happened, I was in Toronto working with the RCMP (Royal Canadian Mounted Police) on a money pickup case up there. My cell phone rang early in the morning in my hotel room. It was Steve Wunderlich calling to tell me that our three fellow agents had just been arrested. Steve told me that when he got to the office that morning there was evidence tape encircling all of our cubicles.

All three agents were immediately suspended pending termination. The first two agents eventually went to trial and were found not guilty on the corruption charge, due to the fact that it was determined that they had been entrapped by the IA agents. They were, however, found guilty of tax evasion for not reporting and paying taxes on the money they allegedly stole. The third agent had quite a different outcome. Several weeks after the initial arrest, he was home getting dressed for a court appearance scheduled for that afternoon. He showered, put on a suit and tie, and sat on the edge of his bed to put on his shoes. His wife was in the kitchen fixing him a cup of coffee before they were to leave for the federal courthouse. He then took out a pistol and placed the barrel of the gun in his mouth and took his own life.

Shortly after graduating from
the Montgomery Police Academy

My beloved bike before it was totaled in an accident

Taking a spin in a Chris-Craft Stinger

On patrol in Biscayne Bay

Preflighting our Customs go-fast before going
out on patrol in the Bahamas for Operation Cat Cay

Taking *Blue Thunder* out for some exercise

Heading out across the Atlantic on some rough seas

Waiting to stop a boat entering US waters

Almost two tons of marijuana
bales on the dock at Papa-100

First-ever joint US-Bahamian
seizure and arrest of smugglers in
Bahamian waters as part of Operation Cat Cay

Arresting two smugglers after a high-speed
boat chase during Operation Hammerhead

Two smugglers posing with the load we
found secreted underneath the deck of their boat

Actor Daniel J. Travanti
after his VIP ride on *Blue Thunder*

A nice catch while "fishing" with my Glock 9mm

A much better "catch." My soon-to-be wife Melissa, an
unauthorized passenger on my Customs cigarette boat

Taking a small bite out of the drug trade in Miami

All in a day's work

Operation Greenback task force seizure

Over $1 million in drug money seized
from a money courier on the streets of Miami

Operation Greenback agents
guarding $22.5 million in cash

US Customs Headquarters wanted to hold a press
conference to bring attention to the record $22.5
million seizure of drug money

Getting ready for the press conference with Woody
Kirk, the best supervisor I ever worked for, and
Steve Hayward, the best investigator I ever knew

More drug profits seized by Operation Greenback

Processing yet another money seizure

Riding a desk at headquarters

US Customs Internal Affairs Headquarters staff in
front of the Ronald Reagan Building in downtown DC

Meeting House Budget Committee Chairman and
Ohio Congressman John Kasich to discuss a
congressional inquiry of US Customs

Getting ready to work an international flight as a US
federal air marshal

Meeting a camel outside of Tel Aviv

The best smoked ribs on the planet can be found at
the Café de Klos in Amsterdam

Some sightseeing in Venice
before working the flight back home

The "Obama Bar" in downtown Barcelona

V. HEADQUARTERS AND THE OFFICE OF INTERNAL AFFAIRS

I WAS TRANSFERRED TO CUSTOMS HEADQUARTERS IN JANUARY OF 1994 and began my tenure there assigned to the Financial Investigations Division. I understood very quickly how different a headquarters assignment was going to be versus a job in the field working actual cases. The freedom of being out every day on my own, working cases in the field with other agents, was now replaced with sitting behind a desk and a computer wearing a suit and tie instead of my usual blue jeans and golf shirt.

I had to give up my government car, as well. Nobody at headquarters had assigned vehicles, so I was going to have to commute every morning. That is when I was introduced to the Slug Line. This was how many people that lived south of Washington, DC, commuted in to work each day. We lived in Woodbridge, Virginia, which was too far south to take the Metro in. I don't know who invented the Slug Line, but it was definitely a brilliant idea and I jumped on it from the beginning. There wasn't available parking at the headquarters building, so driving in was not an option. Even if it was, the traffic going up I-95 was horrendous if you didn't drive in the HOV lanes, which required at least three passengers in a vehicle.

Thus, the invention of the Slug Line. Here's how it worked: I would drive every morning to a large parking lot in Woodbridge near the I-95 on-ramp. People would line up every morning and wait for a car to come through that needed one or two passengers to make the minimum number needed in order to get onto the HOV. Once on the HOV, the traffic moved pretty quickly all the way into DC, stopping at the corner of Constitution and Fourteenth. This just happened to be right in front of the Customs Headquarters building where I worked. The driver would let me out on the corner and I would just get out and walk inside. In the five and a half years I worked at headquarters, the Slug Line never failed to provide me a ride into work.

I was considered a subject-matter expert on undercover money-laundering operations because of what we had been doing in Miami. Because of this, much of my days were spent dealing with all of the field offices throughout the country that had operations similar to Operation FREEZE up and running. Because these types of operations had become so prevalent due to the success coming out of the Miami office, some of the bosses at headquarters determined that a panel needed to convene to write rules and regulations that were needed to govern such operations. I was selected to sit on this panel and help write these rules. Because undercover operations like these could not operate without the use of informants, controlling how and why POI (purchase of information) payments were made to informants was critical to the reforms that were needed. I had processed dozens of POI payments in the past, and in all my cases there were direct seizures related to the payments I made to my informants.

Some of the offices, however, had become lax in their justification for making payments to informants. I remember reviewing a POI request that had come from one of our field offices where the controlling agent had requested what he referred to as "walking-around" money for one of his informants. I called the agent who had sent the request to headquarters and asked what he meant by "walking-around money." I explained to him that POI payments were supposed to be for specific information provided by an informant that directly led to a seizure of some kind.

He told me that he had made similar requests in the past and that they had always been approved before. He told me that it was important for his informant to have a lot of cash in his pocket so that he always had the appearance of being a big-time doper. I laughed and told him that if his guy wants to appear to be "big time," then he needed to give us a worthwhile seizure and get a POI payment based on the size of the seizure. The potential was certainly there for him to get a sizeable payment. I knew this because I had done just that for my informants. As it turned out, this guy's informant had not given us any seizures of note, but instead had been taking this agent for a ride. I knew right then that our panel had our work cut out for us.

Not everything I saw go on at headquarters was positive. I got a firsthand look at the politics that seemed to always be in play. Headquarters positions could be influential from the standpoint that a lot of requests from field offices had to go through somebody's desk in Washington. I saw people at headquarters intentionally sabotage what agents in field offices were trying to get done because of personal differences. Probably the most egregious example of this was what I saw done by a high-ranking director that served as the chief of staff for our ultimate boss, the assistant commissioner of enforcement (the top special agent in all of Customs).

The chief of staff of whom I speak was someone I knew only casually. From my brief experiences with him, I can say unequivocally that he was anything but a decent human being. He held many grudges and was not shy about using his position to screw with as many of his enemies as he could.

One of the things that all Customs agents did when we were hired was to sign what was known as a "mobility agreement." Essentially what this agreement said was that we were required to accept any transfer to any office in the US that the agency deemed was "in the best interest of the agency." In other words, we could be transferred anywhere, at any time, with or without our consent. Most of the time agents were transferred to other offices (or to headquarters) because they had put in for it, either for a promotion or just a change in scenery. This guy, however, couldn't care less about what some agents wanted, especially if they were enemies of his.

If he ever found out that there was a particular office that you did NOT want to work in, and he didn't like you, then the chances were pretty good that that is exactly where you would be transferred. The "directed transfer" letter that was issued to an agent when a transfer was made was a one-page letter that stated: "You have been transferred to the following office: (fill in the blank). Your report date is: (usually ninety days from the date of the transfer letter). Check the box that applies and then sign and return this letter to the chief of staff." The option boxes given to check were: "I accept this transfer and will report on the stated date," or "I refuse this transfer and resign immediately," or "I refuse this transfer with the understanding that if I do not report as directed I will be terminated."

There was a married couple at headquarters during the time I was there that the chief of staff was not too friendly with. The husband was a longtime adversary of his and he wanted to screw with him as much as he could. So he force-transferred his wife to an office out west while leaving him at headquarters. There was absolutely no good reason for separating this agent from his wife and kids except for the fact that this guy just didn't like him. He truly was an abhorrent individual.

One of the things I missed while at headquarters was getting to travel for case-related work. Occasionally headquarters agents got to travel, but the trips were few and far between. One of the regular trips I did get was a teaching assignment at the Customs academy in Arizona. I used to go out there to teach a one-hour block of instruction on financial investigations. The way the federal government worked was you were always granted a travel day on the day before your assignment and a travel day back the day after your assignment. In my case, that meant that if I was going to teach my one-hour class on Wednesday, I would travel on Tuesday, teach my class on Wednesday, and then travel back home on Thursday—all for a one-hour workday on the day I taught my class. Of course, since the class was in Arizona, I always flew out early on travel day, leaving me time to play golf on that day. I would then teach my class the following morning and have time to play that afternoon. The next morning, I would get one more round in before flying back home on an afternoon flight. Did someone say, "Boondoggle?"

Another cool headquarters trip I got was to attend a money-laundering conference being held at Interpol in Lyon, France, as the representative for US Customs. I had always seen TV coverage of UN meetings and how people sat around with headphones on, listening to the translation of what the speaker was saying. This was how the Interpol conference was run. There was a large room with probably a hundred or so chairs, each with their own set of headphones. Behind us were separate soundproof rooms behind glass where translators sat behind microphones, translating what was being said on stage and broadcasting the translation through the headphones located at each chair. I pretty much got nothing out of the conference, but the whole experience was really cool.

Headquarters Christmas parties were something to behold. Looking back on them now, it is amazing that they took place in the manner in which they did. Consumption of alcohol while on duty was absolutely prohibited. However, for the yearly Christmas party the Office of Internal Affairs would always issue a waiver of that prohibition that would essentially make it okay for office parties to take place in the headquarters building where alcohol was served. Fifty-gallon trashcans would be set up on every floor filled with either "hunch-punch" or iced-down beer. On party day, regular work would usually end at noon and the drinking would begin. By four o'clock there would be agents and other personnel who could not walk up and down the hallways without bouncing off the walls. Even worse, almost all of the agents were armed or had their guns stored in their desk drawer. Not smart.

A couple of years after I had transferred to headquarters, these Christmas parties stopped (at least the wanton serving of alcohol ceased). This was in no small part due to what happened in my old task force office in Miami, where I had worked prior to my transfer to Washington. We used to have Christmas parties down there, too, where alcohol was also served. What happened then was an unbelievable tragedy. Someone had brought in "Jell-O shots," which were small Jell-O cubes made with vodka instead of water. There was a DEA agent assigned to my old task force there who had apparently consumed a large number of these Jell-O shots and, according to a friend of mine who was there, was "drunk off his ass."

One of the supervisors in the office rightly pointed out that there was no way they could let this guy drive his government vehicle home. Someone would have to drive him home and he would have to leave his government car at the office and retrieve it the next day after sobering up. A fellow DEA agent volunteered to take his buddy home. On the way home, the drunken agent, sitting in the front passenger seat, apparently had some kind of psychotic episode. He drew his gun from his waistband and began firing at his friend who was driving the car. The guy was killed instantly and the car veered off the road and crashed into a tree.

When first responders arrived at the scene, they later reported that the guy who did the shooting was so drunk that he had no idea what had happened, didn't know how he got there, and couldn't remember anything about what he had just done. Needless to say, I don't think there was ever another party of any kind where alcohol was served (at least not one that was agency sanctioned).

In 1996, I received a headquarters promotion to the US Customs Office of Internal Affairs (IA). This was the part of Customs that agents generally hated. The purpose of their existence was to investigate other Customs employees that were suspected of corruption or any type of wrongdoing. The majority of agents most certainly didn't have a problem with rooting out truly dirty agents. None of us wanted to be tarnished by a fellow agent that was corrupt. Unfortunately, IA had a reputation for going after agents for ridiculous stuff, things that didn't rise to the level of corruption. I had seen fellow agents get in trouble over really minor infractions or just plain honest mistakes—not true corruption. I vowed that I would never become "that" person. I did not want to ever use my position to harm another agent's career unless it was truly a serious infraction. I believe I honored that vow during the time I spent in IA.

My area of responsibility during part of my IA assignment was to oversee the activities of all of the Customs IA offices in the west and southwest. Corruption on the Mexican border had become a problem, with reports of Customs and Immigration inspectors taking bribes from dope smugglers attempting to run loads of drugs into the US via the Customs checkpoints in Texas, Arizona, and California. I participated in a joint effort between US Customs, DEA, FBI, and the US Justice Department to write an operational undercover plan to combat this issue. After weeks of meetings at the Department of Justice building in downtown Washington, DC, and several trips to the border to confer with my IA offices that would be tasked with the plan's implementation, it was finalized.

"Operation Clean Line" was a long-term undercover integrity investigation targeting corrupt government officials (federal, state, and local) that we believed were taking bribes to help dopers facilitate the smuggling of cocaine into the US across the Mexico-US border. This operation, which I oversaw on behalf of Customs Headquarters IA, ended up nabbing several Border Patrol agents, Customs inspectors, and a couple of Arizona Deputy Sheriff's officers who were all shown to have accepted cash payments to "look the other way" as dopers transported drugs into the US.

Each week, the entire IA staff held meetings to discuss outstanding IA cases as well as any new cases that had been opened since the last meeting. This was always an eye-opening endeavor. It was amazing to see the types of situations that Customs employees got themselves into that could potentially lead to them getting suspended or even fired. Someone told me early in my career that the two things that are most likely to get an agent fired are women and informants. Getting too close to either could lead an agent to do something they wouldn't normally do.

I remember discussing the case of an agent who accepted a pair of basketball shoes from an informant. He ended up losing his job over a hundred-dollar pair of sneakers.

There once was a case on a Customs agent assigned to one of our offices on the Mexican border. He had been summoned by INS (Immigration and Naturalization Service) to interview a woman who had been detained at the border attempting to enter the US from Mexico. Following the interview, the agent, apparently enamored with this young lady, talked her into accompanying him back to his house, where they then spent the next two days in bed, apparently taking only small breaks to order takeout and make fresh batches of margaritas. All of this came to light when she contacted IA about a month later to complain that this agent had gotten her pregnant and now refused to return her calls. He ended up getting fired.

Yet another pair of agents lost their jobs after filing their official travel vouchers for a trip they had taken together. They shared a hotel room while on the trip and then filed separate vouchers, claiming reimbursement for a hotel stay for each of them. They were simply going to split the reimbursement for the hotel room not used. They were both fired for voucher fraud, essentially losing their jobs over a couple hundred bucks! Most government people that I worked with and saw on a daily basis were good, dedicated employees. But some were just plain stupid.

Besides the obvious cases of corruption that I saw while working in the Internal Affairs office at headquarters, I also got to see how senior-level managers were treated when they got into trouble. Unfortunately, there were occasions when high-ranking officials did not receive the same level of scrutiny for their "bad" behavior that lower-ranking employees would have gotten.

There was once a high-ranking manager in one of our northeast field offices that was arrested for domestic violence. He apparently had gotten into a physical argument with his teenage daughter and pushed her to the ground, breaking her collarbone. His wife called the police and had him arrested. This was a guy that I had worked with some years earlier in Washington and not someone I had any respect for. I once saw him viciously berate a secretary over some meaningless issue, causing her extreme embarrassment. After she left the room, I told him that his behavior was inexcusable and that he was way out of line for how he had treated her. He didn't appreciate my input and never forgot it.

Like my "friend" Marcy from my Miami days, he was also basically what I would call a black militant. The only white people he had any use for were the ones that outranked him and could be useful to him in his desire to move up the promotion ladder, or those subservient to him that exhibited blind loyalty. In addition to being a first-class A-hole, he was also allegedly carrying on an affair with a young lady in his office that was an administrative assistant. She was convinced that the two of them were in love and was under the impression that he was going to divorce his wife and marry her. Her direct supervisor was a friend of mine and told me that she had come to him one day crying and obviously very distraught because he seemed to be losing interest in her. As it turned out, she ended up quitting after having what some would consider a nervous breakdown.

After the domestic violence issue, headquarters immediately transferred him to another office in California, hoping that a change of scenery would make the problem go away. His wife decided to divorce him and move to another state instead of going with him to California. He ended up beating the criminal charges against him when his daughter refused to cooperate with the prosecution. His direct supervisor in Washington was a friend of mine, and I remember telling him that if they did not drop the hammer on him for his actions, it would come back to haunt the agency. They pretty much swept it under the rug and, unfortunately but not surprisingly, my prediction came true.

A few months after his reassignment, he supposedly got into a shouting match with a female secretary in his new office and grabbed her around the throat. When she reported this to Internal Affairs, Customs Headquarters had had enough. He was forced to retire and left the agency in shame. The fact that the bosses at headquarters allowed him to retire without taking more forceful action against him did not surprise me one bit.

Customs had a reputation for doing this, especially when dealing with high-ranking officials. The most blatant example of this I ever heard of was how they handled a situation that occurred in one of our offices in the southeast region. The agent-in-charge of that office, a guy I had worked with several years earlier in Miami, had gone to a local mall one Saturday afternoon. While sitting in the food court area, he allegedly exposed himself to a teenage girl who happened to be sitting by herself at the table next to him. She immediately reported this to the police. The local police and Customs IA began an investigation. The security tapes were looked at and confirmed that the young girl's assertion was indeed accurate. This guy was transferred back to headquarters, where he was allowed to just occupy a desk for several months until he became eligible to retire.

Everyone that pursues a career in law enforcement knows from the beginning that doing one's job will sometimes involve substantial risk, particularly when the job includes working undercover and posing as a bad guy to the people that are the target of an investigation. An undercover agent working a case knows that at some point in the investigation, he or she will have to make their true identity known to the bad guy when it becomes time to make the arrest. That's the point at which the agent's safety is at the greatest risk. Presumably, that risk to safety would come from the guy being arrested, not from fellow agents.

Unfortunately, that scenario did not play out that way for an agent I knew from our Newark, New Jersey, office. He had been working undercover on a money-laundering case and had arranged to meet his target in a large public parking lot in front of a high-rise office building in downtown Newark. The other agents on his team were spread out in the parking lot and had positioned themselves so they could watch the agent and the target when they met. The plan was to have the undercover agent meet the target at his car and receive from him a duffel bag that contained several hundred thousand dollars in drug money. Once the bad guy opened the trunk of his car and showed the agent the money, the agent was then supposed to adjust the cap he was wearing, which would signal the other agents to move in and make the arrest.

Everything up to this point had gone according to plan. What happened next was one of the most tragic things I've ever seen in my entire career. The first agent to move in to assist in making the arrest of the target just happened to be the agent's very own supervisor. He pulled his car up directly behind the open trunk where the undercover agent and the target were standing. With his gun already out and in his hand, he quickly opened his driver-side door and jumped out of his car, ready to announce himself and make the arrest. The only problem was he forgot to put his car in park before trying to get out. As he began to step out from behind the wheel, his car continued to move forward and he was knocked off balance when the rear doorframe of his driver-side door lightly struck him in his back. When this happened, he inadvertently pulled the trigger on his handgun and fired a shot that struck his agent in the back. Although the agent survived being shot by his supervisor, the bullet severed his spine, causing him to be permanently paralyzed.

Following this tragic incident, the victim's fellow agents were not about to forgive their supervisor's careless act that put their friend and colleague in a wheelchair for the rest of his life. The bosses in the Newark office, as well as some of the bosses at headquarters in Washington, all feared for the safety of the supervisor. They believed (and for good reason) that if this supervisor was not transferred out of the Newark office as soon as possible, his health and well-being could be jeopardized at the hands of some of the other agents who now viewed him with utter disdain. Instead of firing him, which most people thought was appropriate, he was simply transferred to headquarters, where he was able to go on with the rest of his career.

At some point during my headquarters assignment, this cavalier attitude toward misconduct, especially as it pertained to managers, began to drastically change. It became apparent that allegations of misconduct by Customs employees were going to be taken much more seriously than they had been in the past. President Clinton had recently appointed Former NYPD Commissioner Ray Kelly to be the new US Customs commissioner. Commissioner Kelly was really a no-nonsense type of leader. Gone forever were the days when some misconduct would be overlooked. Like, for example, a former special-agent-in-charge who used to leave his office at the end of the day and visit a local pub nearby. Two or three times he was stopped by the local police for DUI in his government vehicle but was never disciplined.

Or the case of what happened to an agent friend of mine in Miami around this same time. He got on the Customs radio around midnight one Saturday night and asked dispatch to have the duty agent on call that evening come and pick him up. He said that the Florida State Troopers had him stopped along the side of the road on I-95 and would not let him leave in his government car because he was DUI. He put this out on the radio! The duty agent responded to the scene and the trooper let my friend go without arresting him for the DUI. Nothing happened to him. Under Commissioner Kelly, stuff like this would no longer be tolerated.

Commissioner Kelly's wrath against Customs employees was never more apparent than when he lowered the boom on about twenty employees who worked in the El Paso region. There was a process in place that all Customs offices followed pertaining to the handling of evidence. Specifically, as in this case, the handling of drug evidence. Seized drugs had to be stored in facilities where the highest levels of security were maintained. The drug evidence would remain secured in this manner until it was needed for court and presented as evidence in a trial. Once the trial was over, sometimes many months or even years from the date the drugs were originally seized, the drugs would be "tagged" for disposal. With the amount of drugs that were being seized at the Mexican border, some of the seizure vaults in the offices along the border would have massive amounts of drugs no longer needed for court and due for destruction.

The procedure for the destruction of drug evidence in the El Paso region was fairly simple. Several armed agents would escort the truck (or trucks) transporting the drugs from the seizure warehouse to a burn facility that Customs had leased. The El Paso burn facility was located outside of town in a fairly remote area with nothing around it for miles. The procedure dictated that upon arrival, agents and seizure clerks would transfer all of the drugs from the truck (in this case almost five tons of marijuana) to the burn room. Once inside, the mounds of marijuana would be doused with kerosene and then set ablaze. After the marijuana was fully engulfed in flames, the door would be locked and agents would wait outside. Someone was supposed to then go inside after the fire was out to make sure that everything was burned up. This was the part that they apparently forgot. After locking the door, everybody there just figured that since the fire was raging, there really wasn't any further need to hang around. So they all left.

Whether someone (or several some ones) was in the woods watching or just happened to be passing by, nobody ever knew. But shortly after all the Customs people vacated the area, the lock to the door was broken and what the fire had not already consumed was stolen. When word of this got back to Washington, DC, Commissioner Kelly lost his mind. He fired everybody. Not just the people who were on site for the destruction, but also everybody that had come in contact with the marijuana that day, including some at the office who helped load the drug evidence onto the truck but were never part of the escort or destruction team. You want to talk about getting someone's attention. Word of this spread like wildfire throughout the agency. Everybody knew that things would be different with this commissioner. The sidenote to this story, however, was the fact that almost all of those fired ended up being reinstated. It took some of them more than two years to get their jobs back, but I'm sure the ordeal was hard on them and their families. Regardless, Commissioner Kelly had made his point.

We sometimes had to find things to amuse ourselves, because it would get tedious at times having to report to a desk every day instead of being in the field like most agents are used to. Jeff Jordan was a fellow agent that worked in IA with me. I decided to play a trick on him just for fun. I usually got to the office every morning before him, so one day I had an idea. Each morning I placed a penny under each of the back legs of his desk. The difference in height that one penny made was not enough for him to notice. However, after about a week and a half of doing this, Jeff could not figure out why every time he laid his pencil down on his desk it would roll off the front.

Brian Smith and John Shirley were two good friends that I had the pleasure and privilege of working alongside for a few years while at headquarters. Brian was smarter than almost anybody I ever worked with and had a very long and very successful federal career in his own right. John was similar in that regard as well.

John was a few years older than Brian and me and used to regale us with stories from his early years in law enforcement. He started his career as a Florida state trooper. My favorite story of his was his recounting of the time he had met a young lady that he became interested in and had definite "designs" on. He asked her if she wanted to go for a ride with him one day while on patrol. His plan was to drive out to Alligator Alley, which at the time was a long deserted stretch of highway in the Florida Everglades, and find some nice, scenic area where they could park and, hopefully, enjoy a romantic encounter. Now I know this was many years ago, but rest assured that cops are still trying this stuff today. Some things will never change.

While on their way, John got a radio call from his shift sergeant who wanted to meet him to discuss some job-related issue. Since having an unauthorized passenger in his patrol car could land him in hot water, John pulled over to the side of the road and asked the young lady to get out and just wait for him to return.

"It should only be a few minutes," he assured her.

The problem was that this was the Florida Everglades. There was swampland on both sides of the highway as far as the eye could see. The highway was named "Alligator Alley" for a reason. Gators, snakes, and other such wildlife were aplenty. This led to a tremendous amount of stress on her part as she envisioned being consumed right there on the side of the road. The other thing prevalent in the Everglades (especially in hot weather, which was most of the time) was mosquitoes. Not just your average-sized mosquitoes either. They were huge.

John finally returned about an hour later. He pulled over to the side of highway and opened the door to let her back in.

"It was the maddest human being I've ever seen in my life," he told us. "She was covered with mosquito bites from head to toe."

Obviously, his plans for a romantic interlude had been seriously damaged. She demanded that he take her back to where her car was and told him never to call her again.

Another great story about John was what happened to him when he was an agent working out of the Charleston, South Carolina, office some years earlier. The Charleston office was located in an old building built around the time of the Civil War and registered on the National Registry of Historic Places. There was a large atrium courtyard area inside the building. All of the interior offices opened out to this area and had metal balconies for walkways between the offices. Due to its historic nature, the building was often used as a backdrop for the film industry.

In 1987, the film *Made in Heaven* was filming on location inside the Charleston US Customs office. The film's production people had printed up several notices and placed them all around the offices asking for everyone to remove their shoes if they were going to be walking on these metal balconies. The notice said that the reason for this was because the noise of walking on the metal balcony would adversely impact the sound quality of the movie being shot. John saw the notice but couldn't care less about some damn movie. He was certainly not going to walk around in his stocking feet because of some stupid notice taped to the wall by these movie people.

He needed to go see his supervisor, so he walked out of his office and made his way around the balcony, the sound of each step reverberating off the metal floor and echoing throughout the atrium. The actress Debra Winger was shooting a scene at that very moment. All of a sudden the director yelled, "Cut!"

Debra Winger looked up at John and yelled, "Goddammit, can't you read, asshole? We're trying to film a movie down here!"

With that John just smiled at her, stepped a little harder, and made even more noise all the way to his boss's office.

The Million Black Man March took place on The Mall during my time at headquarters. My supervisor at the time, Bill Velasco, asked me if I wanted to go with him outside and see all of the marchers.

"Sure, I'll go with you," I said, "but you better make sure you're armed. I don't think we'll be invited to join the march."

The Jew-hating, racist, Muslim Louis Farrakhan was the guy leading this "march." As we walked around amongst the thousands of attendees (nowhere near a million showed up), we got a lot of looks and comments our way, and none of them were positive.

"Hey, look out, here comes the CIA," I heard one march organizer say to us.

Another guy said, "You white boys must be lost."

When I first went to Washington in 1994, the Customs headquarters building was in one of the very old, palatial office buildings located at the corner of Constitution Avenue and Fourteenth Street, across the street from the Washington Monument and two blocks from the White House. This collection of office buildings in DC is known as "The Federal Triangle." We eventually moved over to the newly built Ronald Reagan building, which had been erected right next door. Several other agents and I used to go on runs at lunchtime, usually up and down The Mall, around the Tidal Basin, up the steps of the Capitol, or over the Memorial Bridge to the gates of Arlington National Cemetery. It truly was a great experience to work in our nation's capital.

After five and a half years of riding a desk at headquarters, it was time to move on. I loved my time there, and working at headquarters was definitely a great experience, but I was ready to get back out to the field and get back to working real cases. In the summer of 1999 I was transferred to the Atlanta Field Office. I didn't know it at the time, but this would be my final move.

VI. TIME TO LEAD

OUR FAMILY DECIDED ON LIVING IN PEACHTREE CITY, GEORGIA, A small city about twenty-five miles south of the Atlanta Field Office to which I had been assigned. We bought a new house in a nice part of town and Melissa began getting us settled in, as well as getting our two kids settled in school, Casey in second grade and Kyle in pre-K. I was assigned as the supervisor over the airport group, which was a part of the HIDTA (High Intensity Drug Trafficking Area) Task Force. We worked closely with Atlanta PD, Clayton County PD, and the DEA. Our primary focus was working smuggling cases that emanated from Atlanta's Hartsfield International Airport (ATL) and any other drug or money-laundering cases that fell within the jurisdiction of the Atlanta office. The ATL was the busiest airport in the world and a ripe environment for smuggling ventures.

The lengths that some people went to in order to facilitate the smuggling of drugs into the US was shocking. We began seeing more and more "swallowers" being caught coming in on flights from South and Central America. The swallowers would ingest anywhere from fifty to seventy-five small balloons filled with either cocaine or heroin, fly into the US, and go to a hotel room and just wait for the balloons to pass through their bodies. Once all of the balloons were passed, someone would meet them at their hotel room and take possession of the drugs. They would then board the next flight back home to wherever it was they came from.

Swallowers were usually caught by us at the airport as the result of intensive interviews we would do upon their arrival. Most of the people that agreed to be swallowers were not sophisticated criminals and would usually give themselves away during one of these interviews by being extremely nervous. Once confronted, they would usually admit to having swallowed the drugs that they were carrying inside of them. This is when it really got fun for us. We would take a swallower to Southern Regional Hospital in Clayton County and check them in. I would then assign an agent to round-the-clock duty that included accompanying them into the bathroom with a net whenever they felt the need to have a bowel movement—"Doody duty," as we called it. The agent would then fish through the net and pull out the balloons until all were retrieved. This was truly a "shitty" job, but it had to be done.

After arresting several of these individuals and interviewing them afterward, it became apparent that the drug traffickers were using these people in the worst possible way. Usually poor and with no job, these people would be told by the bad guys that they could make some really good money if they would help them in their smuggling venture and also get to visit the US. When they asked what would happen if they got caught, they were told that if that happened, the US authorities would just seize the drugs they were carrying and then immediately deport them back to the country from which they came. Of course this was nonsense. They would be placed under arrest and would stand trial for drug smuggling. The only way this could be mitigated was if they agreed to cooperate with us and help us further the investigation by helping us identify who their contact was in the US that was supposed to pick up the drugs after they had passed them all.

One time, this guy flew in from Guatemala and had a ticket for a connecting flight from Atlanta to New York City. After showing signs of nervousness in the inspection line, he was pulled into what is known as "secondary," where he could be more intently scrutinized. After a short interview, he admitted to being a swallower and we immediately took him to the hospital. An x-ray was done and the technician brought me in to look at the film. All through his intestinal tract were clear images of little round balloons. There were more than eighty in all. The hospital assigned us a room, and we took him there to wait on Mother Nature to take its course and we could retrieve our dope. Several hours later our swallower began complaining of stomach and chest pains. I asked him if he felt like he needed to go to the bathroom and he said that he had tried but was not able to pass anything. A couple more hours went by with no change in the situation. I called the ER doctor in and he suggested we do another x-ray, which we did.

The new x-ray showed a severe blockage in his intestinal tract that would probably require surgery to relieve. I knew that if this blockage was not corrected, it was entirely possible that one or more of the balloons could rupture inside of him, releasing a massive amount of the drugs (heroin in this particular case) into his bloodstream that would most definitely kill him. I told the doctor to go ahead with the surgery. It was performed with no problems and we were able to retrieve and seize the heroin balloons he had ingested.

What the guy probably didn't realize was that getting caught coming through Customs almost certainly saved his life. Had he made it through undetected, he would have caught his connecting flight to New York and would have gone to the hotel room there that the dopers had reserved for him. At some point in time it would have become evident to the dopers that this guy was never going to successfully pass the balloons (due to the blockage). They simply would have cut him open themselves and retrieved the heroin, leaving him to die on the hotel room floor.

Smuggling ecstasy pills into the US from Amsterdam was very popular and very profitable if you could do it without getting caught. The pills were legal over there and could be bought for about fifty cents per pill. Ecstasy is a psychoactive drug that produces feelings of euphoria and was very popular back then at parties known as "raves." At a typical New York City rave, ecstasy tabs would sell for about thirty to forty dollars per tab. The profit margin was huge if you wanted to take the risk of smuggling them into the US.

We got a tip one day from a DEA agent who told us his informant wanted to "dime out" a former colleague due to the fact that they had some sort of falling-out. The informant told us that his friend would be arriving from Amsterdam into Atlanta and gave us the date he would be arriving. He told us that the guy would be smuggling in a large load of ecstasy and that the pills would be hidden in the shafts of golf clubs. I waited in the Customs arrival section where the baggage was to be retrieved, looking for a set of golf clubs to come through. They arrived along with all of the other bags from that flight, and we just stood to the side and waited for the target to pick his bag up and make his way to the Customs clearance line. When he got in line with the suspect bag, I had a couple of the inspectors pull him out of line and take him to "secondary."

I had already told the Customs inspectors what we were looking for, so they knew right away where we thought the drugs were hidden. I stood over to the side with the guy who just figured it was a routine inspection. As it turned out, the guy was from

Montgomery, Alabama, and was indeed an avid golfer. When I told him that I used to be a cop in Montgomery, he asked if I knew one of his regular golfing mates, a guy named John Jolley.

"As a matter of fact, I know John very well," I told him.

I remembered how much golf John used to play. When one of the inspectors brought out a small handsaw, our target started getting nervous. When the inspector cut through the first shaft, little white pills poured out onto the counter.

The guy looked over at me and said, "Damn, John is going be really disappointed in me."

We ended up seizing about a thousand tabs that day, all hidden inside the hollow shafts of his golf clubs.

Body carriers, as we called them, would simply hide the drugs somewhere underneath their clothing and try to smuggle it in that way. Tight bike shorts with hidden pockets were a very popular method that we saw a lot. We found as many as five or six hundred ecstasy tabs at one time using this method. The really dumb body carriers, however, would come through the inspection line wearing heavy winter coats . . . in the middle of summer! Those were the easy ones.

Sometimes our group worked what is known as a "controlled delivery." If a truck or large vehicle were stopped at the Mexican border and inspectors found it to be laden with drugs, the agents working that case would arrest the suspect and then interview him to see if they could determine where the load was headed. If the subject cooperated and told the agents where they were supposed to take the vehicle, a controlled delivery would be put in motion. Sometimes the load was bound for Atlanta or the surrounding area. In those cases, I would be called and we would participate in the operation.

The way a controlled delivery works is pretty basic. The suspect vehicle would be allowed to leave the border and continue on its intended path. A team of agents would follow the vehicle from the border and coordinate with additional agents all along the intended route. The agents would subsequently "hand off" the suspects to the next set of agents waiting at some predetermined point on the highway, usually at the state line. The controlled delivery vehicle, escorted by a team of agents, would then make their way from the Mexican border all the way to Atlanta (or wherever the intended destination might be). Most of the deliveries like this that we worked ended up being made at a local hotel. We would set up surveillance around the hotel and wait for the suspect vehicle to arrive. We would be in radio contact with the escorting agents so we always knew exactly where the load was and when it was due to arrive. Once it arrived, we would wait for the suspect driver to get out and take the load into one of the rooms. Once inside, we would crash in the door with guns and badges out and make the arrests.

Doing controlled deliveries could be problematic for us agents. Not just because we were dealing with potentially dangerous suspects, but also because we were allowing drugs into the country after initially finding them at the original border stop. It was a big endeavor to make sure agents stayed in contact with the suspect vehicle (and by extension, the drugs) all the way from the Mexican border to another US city, sometimes thousands of miles away. When I spent time in IA at headquarters, we used to convene what was known as the "Lost Load Committee." This committee would review each case where a controlled delivery was attempted but was somehow lost by the agents. The agents were supposed to maintain contact 100 percent of the time, but for whatever reason did not and subsequently lost the load. It didn't happen often, but it did happen. And believe me, you did not want to be the subject of that review.

Working for the government was sometimes much harder than it needed to be. When I first transferred to Atlanta, the boss of the office called me in one day to tell me that he had done everything in his power to have my transfer there rescinded. He told me that he wanted to be the one to pick all of his management positions and that he was "pissed off" that I had been transferred there without his consent. I reminded him that my transfer to Atlanta was a directed reassignment and that we both would just have to make it work.

The airport group I took over had horrible morale problems and was basically not producing any worthwhile cases. That began to change shortly after I arrived. Seizure and arrest stats improved over 300 percent in my first year, but that did nothing to assuage the feelings that my boss had toward me. He undercut my authority every chance he got and tried to make my life as miserable as he could. I just kept my head down and did my job to the best of my ability, in spite of the lack of support I was receiving. To me, this highlights one of the biggest differences between private sector work and working for the government. In the private sector, an employee is generally judged on their ability to produce, coupled with their overall work ethic. The government is far too often the opposite. Too many senior-level managers in the government could not care less about one's level of production. Instead, they too often treat their subordinates in ways that are based on whether they like you or not.

After a couple of years running the airport group, it became apparent to me that this was the toughest and most stressful job I had ever had. I was basically on call 24-7 and would respond to the airport at all times of the day whenever the inspectors made a seizure or arrest. This happened quite a bit in the evenings and over the weekend. I remember going out on a date one night with my wife, Melissa, and sitting down at a nice restaurant for dinner. The kids were young back then, and occasions like this were too few and far between. Before the waiter could take our order, my phone rang and it was the Customs inspection supervisor calling to tell me that they had just made a drug seizure at the airport from someone flying in from Nigeria. Melissa knew that our night was pretty much over and that I was going to have to respond to the airport.

She was really magnificent with her understanding of my job and was not too upset. The restaurant where we were at was not too far from the airport, so I asked her if she wanted to go with me. It took a couple of hours to complete what I needed to do, and she and I then drove back home.

On the way back, I apologized for our date being ruined and added, "But I bet that was the most heroin you've ever seen before."

She laughed and assured me that it most certainly was.

One of the more disgusting crimes that law enforcement agents must address is that of child pornography. It is a real problem in this country. Most child pornography back then was produced in other countries and, therefore, fell under the jurisdiction of US Customs. This was because the pornographic material would have been imported across the US border and into our country, either via the mail or internet. Kiddie porn cases worked out of the Atlanta office of US Customs fell within the purview of my group. Thankfully, we didn't work many of these types of cases, but we did work some. They were all vile and quite disturbing.

One of the targets of a child porn case I worked was a guy that lived in a wealthy part of downtown Atlanta. We got a search warrant for his house and decided on the day and time to serve the warrant. Several agents and I met near his home early one morning and waited for the sun to come up before serving the warrant. Search warrants generally have to be served during daylight hours except when extreme circumstances exist.

When dawn broke, we knocked on the front door and shouted, "Federal agents with a search warrant," and then crashed in the front door and entered.

With guns drawn, we quickly moved through the house looking for the occupant, who just happened to be taking a shower at the time. I heard the shower running and pushed open the door to his bathroom and again announced myself. The guy pushed aside the shower curtain and immediately saw me pointing my weapon directly at him. He was obviously stunned. I told him to towel off and put on his robe and then ordered him to accompany us on our search of his home. We ended up seizing several boxes of VCR tapes, his computer, and hundreds of pages of printed material, much of which contained the most disgusting images you can imagine. Without a doubt, these cases were the most unenjoyable criminal cases I ever worked, but they had to be worked nonetheless.

VII. THE FEDERAL AIR MARSHALS AND THE WINDING DOWN OF A CAREER

SEPTEMBER 11, 2001, WILL BE REMEMBERED AS ONE OF THE MOST devastating days in our country's history. Terrorists took over four commercial airplanes, flying two of them into the World Trade Center in New York, one into the Pentagon, and crashing the fourth in a field in Pennsylvania after passengers fought back against their hijackers. I was sitting in a hotel conference room in Norfolk, Virginia, attending a conference when the first plane hit the towers. A fellow supervisor walked into the conference room and informed us all that she had just been looking at a TV in the hotel lobby that showed an airplane flying into the World Trade Center. She said that the reporter had described it as a terrorist attack. The conference was cancelled and we all got in our rental cars and immediately drove back to Atlanta.

By the time we got back to Atlanta, it was confirmed that our country was definitely under attack by terrorists. I immediately reported to my office at the Atlanta airport, which was eerily quiet because all air traffic in the US had been temporarily halted. We knew air traffic would eventually be restored, so we needed a game plan for how we were going to react once it was reestablished.

"Profiling" has become a dirty word in the world of law enforcement. It basically means that agents and officers target a group of people for extra scrutiny based solely on their ethnicity. This is exactly what we did. When air traffic throughout the US was restored, I ordered my agents to retrieve every passenger manifest for each and every international flight that was scheduled to leave or arrive at Hartsfield International Airport. Once we got a copy of these manifests, we highlighted every name that appeared to be Arab and pulled these people to the side to conduct extensive interviews. We did this for all outbound or inbound international flights. Nothing of note came out of this extra scrutiny, but in hindsight, I will note that not a single person objected or expressed any disfavor with what we were doing. On the contrary, I remember several of the individuals stating to me that they completely understood why we were targeting them and how much they hated what had happened.

I stayed on in my role over the airport group for the next several months as I watched the changes being made in federal law enforcement due to the September 11th attacks. Up until then Customs agents fell under the US Treasury Department. Following 9/11, they would be reassigned to the newly created Department of Homeland Security (DHS). Another change being implemented was the creation of the Federal Air Marshal Service (FAMS), which would be a part of DHS and would be a direct response to the hijackings that took place. I considered the possibility of moving over to the FAMS, because I knew that if I stayed with US Customs I would not be able to finish my career in Atlanta.

It was very common for managers to be rotated from office to office, and it was going to be nearly impossible for me to stay in Atlanta before reaching retirement eligibility. My parents had moved within a few miles of us, and I was doing more and more to help look after my father whose health was deteriorating. Additionally, Melissa's father, whose health was also in decline, had moved in with us so she could better care for him. Another move was definitely not in the best interest of our family, as we had become quite settled in the Atlanta area. It was primarily for this reason that I agreed to accept a transfer over to the newly formed Atlanta FAMS office in June of 2002.

Air marshals existed prior to 9/11, but in extremely low numbers. When terrorists attacked us on that fateful day, there were less than forty air marshals in existence. At that time, they were all based out of New Jersey, where the Federal Aviation Administration, or FAA, flight training center was housed, and flew primarily on international flights. That all changed after 9/11. Through an act of Congress, a new agency was created known as the Federal Air Marshals Service. The federal government is historically known for its inability to do much in a timely fashion or with much efficiency, but this new agency was needed NOW and would have to be staffed with a cadre of armed personnel essentially overnight.

The only way to accomplish this was to staff the agency primarily with federal agents from other agencies. These agents were already trained, had already passed background investigations, and could be assigned to work commercial flights immediately. Many local police officers were also hired in the early days, but they would be required to go through a two-month training academy before getting their flight assignments. As a current special agent with US Customs, I only had to attend a one-week orientation before I got my first flight assignment.

The first air marshals to fly armed on commercial flights actually began back in the early '60s. Back then they were known as sky marshals. This program was initiated by then-President Kennedy as a direct response to a new problem that had emerged, namely, the hijacking of US flights. At that time, Cuban nationals had hijacked a number of flights and forced the pilots of those planes to fly them to Cuba. There wasn't the creation of a new agency, just the temporary reassignment of a small number of federal agents to protect flights that were possible targets of potential hijackers. Over the next few years, these agents eventually went back to the agencies from which they came and the sky marshal program substantially disappeared. That is, until about 1968 when a new rash of hijackings began to take place.

Around 1970, the US Customs Service took about 1,800 of its agents and reassigned them as sky marshals. But again, this was not the creation of a sky marshal or air marshal agency, just the reassignment of duties for these federal agents. The reason that this is important, and how it was vastly different than what happened after 9/11, was due to the fact that as quickly as these Customs agents were reassigned to sky marshal duties, they could just as quickly be reassigned back to their former duties and taken out of the skies. Sometime around 1973, the FAA began screening passengers using metal detectors before being allowed to board flights. Because of this, it was felt back then that the need for a large contingent of sky marshals no longer existed. The sky marshal force gradually dwindled to only about 400, and through attrition over the next several years, the number of sky marshals fell to less than forty, which is where it was on 9/11. The creation of a Federal Air Marshal Service after 9/11 put in place a permanent force of undercover, gun-carrying agents whose sole assignment was the protection of commercial aircraft from the threat of hijacking.

As with most everything in life (and especially in the federal government), there was a lot of both good and bad with this new agency. The focus on training that was established was second to none. The firearms proficiency standards of a FAM are higher than that of any other federal agent in the government. This was for good reason. If an air marshal was going to stop a terrorist attack onboard an aircraft (as what happened on 9/11), he or she would be required to fire their weapon in the close quarters of an airplane where hundreds of innocent passengers were seated. Expert marksmanship on the part of a FAM was not just preferred, it was essential.

We also went through extensive training pertaining to the recognition of potential terrorists and close-quarter self-defense tactics. We also practiced arrest techniques that would need to be utilized within the small confines of an airplane cabin. Probably the most concentrated training regimens that we practiced every few months were how to best coordinate with fellow air marshals the tactics that would be necessary for us to establish control and dominance over a would-be hijacker (or hijackers) once they exhibited their intentions of taking over a flight at thirty-five thousand feet. These were always by far the most intense portions of our training.

Air marshals sometimes travel in teams, and good coordination is imperative. We had to know what the other FAM was thinking, and more importantly, what the other FAM would do once the proverbial "stuff" hits the fan. Make no mistake about it; the FAMS are the most highly trained outfit in all of federal law enforcement.

Because federal law enforcement agents deal with what's known as "law-enforcement-sensitive" information, we are required to maintain a "top secret" clearance level. I had that clearance throughout my entire federal career. Even though I am now retired, I am still obligated by law not to reveal anything that is considered to be law-enforcement-sensitive. Because of this, I can only write in general terms of what the duties of an air marshal encompass, including what flights are covered and why.

Suffice to say that the assignment of air marshals on commercial flights is not done randomly. The agency goes to great lengths when deciding what flights are assigned for air marshal coverage and why. With over thirty thousand daily commercial flights in the US, it would be impossible to have coverage on each one. The team at FAMS headquarters that is responsible for the assignment of flights works meticulously 24-7 to make sure the flying public is protected whenever and wherever it is deemed necessary.

Unfortunately, the task of putting together a cadre of several thousand air marshals almost overnight came with some inherent risks as well. Namely, bringing people on board that simply were not equipped for the job, like one FAM I knew of that had what some would consider a nervous breakdown while on an international flight. I was not on this flight, but a good friend who was told me how they found him in the lavatory weeping, distraught over the fact that, according to him, no one liked him and that other FAMs did not want to fly with him. The other

FAMs on the flight ended up taking his gun away and made him stay in his seat until the flight arrived back in the US.

Another great example of hiring was the FAM who was hired and assigned to a FAM field office on the east coast. His very first mission was a flight to a major city on the west coast. After arriving, he checked into his hotel room for the night to await his return home the following morning. Once in his room, he went through the yellow pages and found an ad for an escort service and promptly placed a call asking them to send a young lady over to his room. This escort promptly showed up and knocked on the hotel room door. After this FAM let her in, she went into the bathroom to change. A few minutes later she came out and found this FAM sitting in a chair, wearing nothing but his law enforcement tactical badge hanging from a chain around his neck. After they concluded their night's activity, the FAM told her that he could have her arrested, but if she would just leave quietly nothing more would come of it. In other words, he was going to stiff her the money he owed her. She immediately went downstairs to the lobby and called the police. When they showed up, she told them everything that happened and they promptly went upstairs and arrested him. He was immediately fired and had to pay for his own ticket to get back home.

There were two FAMs overnighting in a major US city once that thought it would be a good idea to visit a topless bar located near their hotel. They went inside, found a table, and ordered some drinks. After enjoying the show and consuming several more drinks, they got into a verbal altercation with two other patrons. These guys were apparently much bigger than the FAMs and probably more inebriated. The altercation turned physical when one guy knocked one of the FAMs to the ground, causing the other FAM to pull out his weapon and threaten to shoot them if they didn't back away. Obviously, drinking alcohol while armed is verboten and grounds for immediate dismissal. They ran out of the place, but not before someone inside called the police. The cops caught up to them and they were arrested. They too were immediately fired.

One of the more bizarre stories I heard happened to a FAM from one of our Midwest offices. The FAM team had worked an international flight to a major European city where it just so happens that prostitution is legal. At least two of the FAMs decided to visit one of the local brothels after having dinner that night. After securing the services of one of their "hosts" and concluding their activity, this FAM noticed the unusually large Adam's apple on the "woman" whose services he had just procured. After realizing that this "woman" was actually not a woman, he went crazy, refused to pay, and generally caused a big disturbance that got everybody's attention. The local police were called and the other FAMs that were on the trip with him felt the need to report what had happened to their supervisors back in the US, no doubt trying to protect their own jobs. Why this guy just didn't keep his mouth shut about the whole ordeal and take what happened to him to his grave with him will always be a mystery.

Then there was the FAM who worked a mission to another major European city. After returning to his hotel from dinner, he walked through the lobby of his hotel and spotted a purse that someone had left behind on a chair. He looked around to see if anyone else was in the lobby and when he didn't see anybody, opened the purse and took out about two hundred euros. He then went upstairs to his room. The lady whose purse it was came down some time later to retrieve it, and when she noticed her money was missing, reported it to the desk clerk. The clerk then called the local police who responded to the hotel and asked the desk clerk to show them the videotape of the camera that was in the lobby area. It showed the FAM stealing the money, and they immediately went to his room and arrested him.

He claimed he was "holding it for safe keeping." The local cops didn't believe him but since he was an American law enforcement officer over there on official business, they opted to release him to one of the other FAMs. When the incident was reported back to FAM headquarters, the particular FAM in question was told to relinquish his weapon to the team leader on the mission and subsequently had to purchase his ticket for the return flight. He was relieved of duty when he got back. I suppose there are bad apples in every line of work or profession. The FAM Service, unfortunately, surely had their fair share and a few extras.

In my twelve years as a FAM, I flew a total of about 3.5 million miles (and no, I did not get to claim frequent flyer miles). I never encountered a hijacker, and the only times I took any kind of official action was to deal with the occasional idiot or drunk that decided to "show his ass" on a flight by causing a disturbance or giving the flight attendants a hard time. I never once had to pull out my badge and officially identify myself, but almost everybody knew of the existence of air marshals. The times I did step in to help defuse a situation, I'm pretty sure the other person had a good idea of who I was.

Once on a shuttle flight from Washington, DC, to New York, I sat across the aisle from New York Senator Chuck Schumer. The flight attendant announced on the PA that we were getting ready to take off and for all phones to be turned off. Senator Schumer had been on his phone since boarding began and he apparently wasn't finished with his call. After her third announcement, everybody around us was looking at him and he was still talking. Schumer is a far-left Democrat and someone in the political arena that I pretty much loathe. I unbuckled my seatbelt and stood up in the aisle next to his chair and leaned in close to his face.

I got about ten inches from his face and said very sternly, yet quietly, "Hey, asshole, turn your damn phone off!"

I'm quite sure it had been a long time since anyone had spoken to him like that. He immediately turned off his phone and looked down at his newspaper that was in his lap, not wanting to maintain eye contact with me in any way. He didn't say a word to me the remainder of the flight.

The shuttle flights between DC, New York, and Boston were frequent flights that all air marshals work on a regular basis for obvious reasons. Waiting in the boarding area for one of these flights, I noticed that the journalist George Stephanopoulos was booked on my same flight. The gate agent had just announced a delay due to a mechanical issue and everyone waiting just seemed to sigh in frustration, knowing they were going to be late. We didn't really care about delays. We were getting paid to be there and it didn't really matter to us if we were late or not. I walked over to the window for a moment and then back to the seating area where George and everybody else was seated. Someone asked me if I saw anything that would indicate what the problem was.

I then jokingly said, "I'm not sure, but the mechanics are out there wrapping duct tape around one of the wings!"

Stephanopoulos dropped the paper he was reading and frantically sat up in his chair.

"They're doing what?" he asked incredulously.

The look on his face was hilarious. He actually believed me. I just smiled and said I was kidding and a few of the people just laughed. Not George.

On another shuttle flight, I was seated next to Placido Domingo, an international singing star and one of the famed Three Tenors. For the entirety of the forty-minute flight he looked out his window and quietly sang, just loud enough that only I, and possibly the guy in front of him, could hear. I can always claim that I was privy to a private concerto by an internationally famous singer.

Another somewhat famous singer I encountered was LL Cool J (now a TV actor). When I boarded the plane, I moved into the first-class section where my seat was and as I approached it, noticed someone in my assigned seat. When I reached my aisle, LL stood up and asked if I would mind swapping seats with him so that he could sit by his friend who was already seated in the window seat next to LL I asked what seat and he pointed to the bulkhead window seat a few rows up.

Normally, I never minded swapping seats with people so that they could sit with a friend or family member. In this case, however, I did not want to sit in the bulkhead window seat because it was not a tactically sound seat to be in should anything bad happen on the flight. I wanted to be on the aisle with as much of an unobstructed sightline as possible to the flight deck. I told him sorry but that I did not want to move. LL was very "cool" about it and turned to his friend and told him that he was going to have to get up and move.

The guy immediately tried to stand but had forgotten that he already had fastened his seatbelt. In addition to that, he was holding a large Starbucks coffee with the lid removed. When he tried to stand his seatbelt grabbed and pulled him back down into his seat, causing him to overturn the entire cup of coffee into what was supposed to be my seat. We ended up taking a delay so that the flight crew could have the seat cushion replaced because it was too soaked with coffee for anyone to sit in. As I stood up front waiting for the cushion to be replaced, I couldn't help but notice all the sneers I was receiving due to the fact that everybody pretty much blamed me for the delay because I wouldn't swap seats.

Sometimes I had enjoyable interactions with celebrities I ran into and sometimes not so much. The comedian Tracy Morgan was a trip. He and his girlfriend sat across the aisle from me in first class once. While we waited on the ground for the rest of the plane to be boarded, he basically worked on some of his material with us, cracking jokes and taking pictures with some of the passengers. I remember him announcing that he and his girlfriend were on their way to LA to try out a new enema procedure he had heard about and they were anxious to try it out. His girlfriend just shook her head and constantly looked away in embarrassment.

Jane Fonda was an entirely different story. This washed-up, communist-loving old bag was on a couple of different flights that I worked. Once, after being openly rude to the flight attendant, I saw her remove her shoes and proceed to get up and go into the forward lavatory. If there was one thing I learned from all the flying I did, it was that the floors of airplane lavs are always covered in urine after the first hour or so of any flight. After a few minutes in the lav, she returned to her seat and promptly propped her wet stocking feet on the bulkhead in front of her seat, apparently unaware of the "smear" marks she was leaving behind. She is truly a disgusting individual.

My friend J. T. and I got off a flight in DC and proceeded to walk through the gate area when we noticed Mitt Romney standing beside the wall next to the restrooms. I'm pretty sure he was just waiting for his wife who was inside the ladies' room. Both J. T. and I were fans of Romney and had voted for him earlier that year in the Republican primary (this was during the 2008 election when John McCain beat Romney for the Republican nomination).

J. T. said to me, "Hey, there's Romney. Let's go say hello."

Romney could not have been more rude or more of an A-hole. When he noticed that we had zeroed in on him and were approaching to speak to him, he turned his body in such a way that he was facing the wall and just stared straight ahead at the wall.

I had already extended my hand and said to him as we got closer, "Governor Romney, it's a pleasure to meet you."

Romney continued to gaze at the wall, trying to avoid making eye contact. I noticed this right away but was determined that I would not be dissuaded. I got within a few feet of him and kept my hand extended, indicating I wanted to shake his. After a few seconds of this, he turned his head in our direction and reached out to grab mine, quickly shaking hands while still facing the wall. After a quick shake his eyes diverted back to the wall, obviously anxious for us to leave him alone.

As we walked away, J. T. said, "What an asshole. I'll never vote for that guy again."

The current governor of Virginia, Terry McAuliffe, was probably the nicest political celeb I ever met. Although he was a long-time friend of Bill and Hillary Clinton and an ardent Democrat, I wanted to meet him anyway. I approached him in the gate area before we got on the plane and introduced myself to him. We weren't supposed to tell people who we were, but I figured he wasn't a safety risk. After we boarded, we found our seats beside each other in first class. After some general chitchat, I began reading a newspaper I had and he took out a notebook of some kind that he had brought with him. It was still in the boarding process so his phone was still on. When it rang he pulled it out of his pocket, looked at the number, and then nudged me with his elbow.

"Look at that," he said to me, pointing at his phone. "It's the president."

He then put his phone to his ear and motioned for me to lean in so that I could hear when he hit the "answer" button.

"Hello, Mr. President. Thanks for getting back to me," he said into his phone.

Sure enough as I leaned in to listen, I could hear the unmistakable voice of Bill Clinton on the line. McAuliffe looked up at me with a big smile, pointing to his phone as if to say, "See that? It's really President Clinton on the line."

I never considered my job as an air marshal to truly be a law enforcement job, at least not compared to being a cop in Alabama or my time as a Customs special agent. In those jobs I worked real criminal cases and put people in jail. If an incident of some kind doesn't take place on a flight, an air marshal is pretty much just along for the ride. To be sure, we are there to provide security for the passengers and crew, but the reality is that 99 percent of flights are incident free. I always thought it was a great way for me to finish out my law enforcement career, because it was generally stress free and I got to visit a lot of places that I otherwise would have never traveled to.

My all-time favorite trip was to Tel Aviv, Israel. I went there several times and the highlight of that trip was visiting Old Jerusalem and getting to walk all around the Holy Lands. Visiting the Western (or Wailing) Wall and the Church of the Holy Sepulcher and seeing where Jesus was crucified was phenomenal. I also walked through the Mount of Olives and saw the spot where the Roman guards took Jesus into custody after His betrayal by Judas. It was a truly amazing experience.

My two favorite places in the world to eat are the Café de Klos in Amsterdam and Ye Olde Six Bells near Gatwick Airport in London. Every time I went to either city (and I went to both often), those places were a must. Other incredible things I got to experience that were only possible because of my job were walking across the Charles Bridge in Prague and seeing the Coliseum in Rome, as well as Michelangelo's frescos on the ceiling of the Sistine Chapel. I got to stand in front of da Vinci's painting of The Last Supper in Milan and went to the top of the world's tallest building in Dubai. I also went to a World Cup soccer match in Johannesburg, South Africa, and drove by the home of Nelson Mandela.

On a trip to Edinburgh, Scotland, we rented a car and drove up the coast and visited St. Andrews. The highlight for me was walking around the Old Course at St. Andrews, where the game of golf was essentially invented. I had my picture taken on the Swilcan Bridge, which is near the eighteenth-tee box. I loved the beaches of Barcelona, Spain, and got to see a bullfight in Madrid.

On one of my trips to Munich, Germany, I took a train and visited the Dachau Concentration Camp and saw the ovens used by the Nazis to exterminate their Jewish prisoners. After seeing the movie *Slumdog Millionaire,* I got to visit the real slums of Mumbai, India. I also took a boat up the Grand Canal in Venice and toured the Louvre and Eiffel Tower in Paris. My favorite city of all is probably Bruges, Belgium, an old medieval city outside of Brussels. There's an old clock tower there that dates back to the 1200s that was featured in the movie *In Bruges* (one of my all-time favorites). A circular stoned stairway that's only about two feet wide winds its way up to the top of the tower.

One of the last international trips I took before retiring was probably my least favorite of all. It was to Lagos, Nigeria. This was right around the time when there was worldwide concern about a possible outbreak of Ebola. When we stepped off the plane, an official who was tasked with escorting us through the Nigerian Customs clearance procedures met the other air marshals and me. After clearing us through Customs, he escorted us to an armored vehicle that was used to take us to our hotel.

As we walked through the terminal, this official pointed to a spot on the floor and told us, "Here's where the guy collapsed and died last week from Ebola."

We all just looked at each other with wry smiles.

My two children used to kid me about how easy my job was; that all I did was fly around in first class, reading books and watching movies. I can't say that I didn't do a lot of both, but the life of an air marshal is not nearly as serene as my kids made it seem. The amount of flying that a FAM does in a given year actually takes a heavy toll on one's body. A long time ago, the FAA set limitations for how much time pilots and flight attendants were allowed to fly in a given month. There is a reason for this. These rules, however, do not apply to air marshals. The FAM service tried to limit "fly days" for an air marshal in a given month, but the number of hours a FAM could conceivably be in the air had no limitation. Additionally, if the agency "deemed it necessary," they would just throw out the limitations on "fly days per month" anyway.

It is vitally important for a FAM to stay alert at all times, and for obvious reasons. I never had the luxury (as most passengers do) of just settling back in my seat for the duration of the flight. Even though you know before a flight takes off that it's probably going to be an incident-free mission, you have to stay on your guard at all times regardless. An air marshal must be ready at all times to react to anything that happens on a flight that may need his or her intervention. Because of the level and intensity of the training that we constantly went through, I always felt adequately prepared to handle any issue that would arise. This was due in no small part to the contributions made by those air marshals and others who dedicate themselves to providing us with the most relevant and most applicable training environment possible. What concerned me and other air marshals the most were those situations that could possibly come up on a flight that were completely out of our control.

The best example of this occurred on a flight we had to Stuttgart, Germany. After being in the air for about four hours, we cleared the northern tip of Canada and began to head out over the Atlantic toward Europe. The engine on the starboard wing suddenly burst into flames. For a few seconds our plane looked like a meteorite streaking across the sky before the pilots hit the engine extinguisher and put the fire out. The engine was obviously fried and no longer working, which caused a significant amount of discomfort for most of the passengers (including the FAMs). The pilot came on the PA and informed us that we were turning around and would be landing in Newfoundland, Canada, and that the plane should fly just fine on one engine (note he said "should"). As it turned out, he was right, and we landed about twenty minutes later and everything was fine, but not before experiencing a few moments of sheer terror.

I heard someone say a long time ago that if you can find something that you are passionate about, and you can get paid to do it, you'll never have to work a day in your life. That's kind of how I feel about my career. Now, there certainly were a lot of long workdays, like sitting on surveillance as a Customs special agent around the clock, waiting for someone to move, or flying back from the other side of the world on a seventeen-hour flight. But in hindsight, it just never seemed like work to me because I genuinely loved what I was doing. Society needs dedicated law enforcement officers, and I truly believe that God called me to do just that. He kept me safe every time I got myself in a situation that could have turned out bad, and in my thirty-three-year career of carrying a gun, I had more than my share of those types of situations.

In 2014 I decided that it was time to hang it up. My wife, Melissa, was on board and agreed with me that I had given enough. I'm sure that being the spouse of a law enforcement officer can be trying at times. I know it was with mine. She knew most of what went on and the kinds of things that I was doing on the job. I'm sure that she had more than a few worried moments over the past couple of decades. Besides being blessed by God with a long and satisfying career, I was doubly blessed by having Melissa to share the ride with me. She was always (or at least almost always) understanding about the crazy hours and all of the nights away. If I could go back in time to when I was twenty-one years old, I think I would do just about everything the same way again.

I have no way of knowing why others choose a career in law enforcement. I know with me it was a "calling." I truly believe I was put on this earth by God to do exactly what I did and to be the best law enforcement officer I could be. There are about eight hundred thousand sworn officers at the federal, state, and local level in this country.[*] About a hundred are killed every year in "line-of-duty" incidents. According to FBI statistics, law enforcement officers are assaulted between forty-five and fifty thousand times

---

[*] "Careers in Law Enforcement," LawEnforcementEDU.net, accessed June 1, 2016, http://www.lawenforcementedu.net/.

a year while performing their official duties. And they are doing all of this for a median salary (as of 2012) of $55,000 a year.[†]

There are so many more lines of work a person can pursue that pay much better and are much safer than being a law enforcement officer. But for me, and I suspect most others, it was never about the money. When one is "called" to serve and protect, the potential risks that are inherent to this line of work are just accepted as part of the job. I have no idea what kind of stress those who are accountants, or retail managers, or truck drivers, or lawyers, or doctors, or any other profession encounter. I'm sure it exists for everyone in all lines of work to some degree or another. I just know that with law enforcement officers, the stress of the job can sometimes be all encompassing.

A sworn officer really does put his or her life on the line every day that he or she goes into work. We all know that to be a fact. Many I have seen over the years were not able to handle it, and fortunately for them, they got out to pursue other things. As for me, I cannot see myself in any other career endeavor. Law enforcement has provided me with a way that I could serve my country and my fellow man, as well as provide a decent living by which I could take care of my family. Whatever the risk—and there were many—it was all worth it. I was blessed beyond measure to be able to live out my dream.

[†] "Salaries," LawEnforcementEDU.net, accessed June 1, 2016, http://www.lawenforcementedu.net/salaries/.

About the Author

DAVID COPPAGE WAS BORN AND RAISED IN MIAMI, FLORIDA. HE obtained his bachelor's degree in criminal justice from Troy University in Troy, Alabama, in 1981. In 1985 he received his master's degree in criminal justice from Troy University, Montgomery, Alabama. He currently resides in Senoia, Georgia, with his wife, Melissa, where he is a real estate agent with Keller Williams of Newnan.

To purchase additional copies of this book, please
visit the author's website at www.davidcoppage.com.